tana ramsay's family kitchen

Simple and delicious recipes
for every family

HarperCollins*Publishers*

For my mum and dad.
I hope my children grow up with the same
sense of love and comfort that you gave me.
Thank you.

HarperCollins*Publishers*
77–85 Fulham Palace Road
Hammersmith, London W6 8JB

The website address is: www.harpercollins.co.uk

First published by HarperCollins 2006
This edition published 2008

10 9 8 7 6

Photographs © Deirdre Rooney

Styling: Wei Tang
Food styling: Jenny White

A catalogue record of this book is
available from the British Library

ISBN-13   978-0-00-722577-4
ISBN-10   0-00-722577-6

Printed in China by
South China Printing Co. Ltd

contents

introduction

I must admit that I hardly cooked until I had children. Gordon was always working until at least midnight and I was working all day and studying for my teaching course in the evening – I became a Montessori nursery teacher. I more or less lived on quick and easy foods like beans on toast or breakfast cereal. My interest in food only really started when we had children and our first, Megan, began solids. Suddenly I was responsible for everything that went into her tiny tummy. Gordon was working and it was up to me to cook for her. That was when I started to really care about what was in the fridge.

I learnt how to cook as Megan's diet became more interesting than vegetable purées. The fact that she was a good eater and showed excitement in what she ate, as subsequently did the other three, meant I actually enjoyed experimenting, too. So that is how I started cooking – never seasoning or overcomplicating, just simple, family food. I believe home cooking never needs to be any more sophisticated than this.

I've tried to keep the recipes in this book as real and accessible as possible. I've included all of my favourites that I use to feed the family, which also means that they have been given the thumbs up by the children. Some of the recipes are more child-oriented – like fish fingers, for example – but most of them are for the whole family to enjoy.

I've also tried to include tips on how to adapt some of the recipes to make them more adult. A splash of wine or a bit of extra seasoning is often all it takes. Not only does this save you the time and effort of cooking two different meals, but it also makes eating, especially at weekends, as much about being together as a family as eating good food. That for me is just as important.

The recipes are organized with most people's weekly routines in mind. In the Breakfasts section, for example, I've included a mixture of quick and easy options for weekdays when you are rushing to get the kids to school as well as a few more leisurely recipes for weekends and holidays. The most popular with my children is probably the fruit gratin, so if you can't quite squeeze it into a busy weekday morning, do indulge at the weekend. I've organized main meals into After-school Suppers and Weekend Lunches for the same reason.

I also thought a section on Cooking from the Cupboard was essential. If you are anything like me, sometimes you are just too busy, tired or disorganized to get to the supermarket and you end up staring at the contents of the fridge and cupboards trying to figure out what to feed everybody. I do try to keep a few staples in the house at all times, a few of which I have outlined at the beginning of that chapter. If you can get into the habit of keeping all of these in stock then you'll find it actually quite easy to rustle up something delicious.

I actually find cooking *ad hoc* makes me more creative as I match flavours and ingredients that I might not normally. With this chapter, if you don't have a particular item you can often substitute it for something else. I have tried to include notes on how you could do this in a number of the recipes throughout the book. For example, I really enjoy cooking with pancetta, but if you can't get hold of it, you can substitute unsmoked streaky bacon or bacon lardons. Don't be afraid to experiment! It's how we all learn and more often than not it'll go down well.

This is also why I've included a section on Trying New Tastes. Children – and mine are no exception – can have very fixed ideas of what they think they like and dislike, when quite often they only need a food presented to them in a different way or just as a sneaky aside to other things they know they already love. The recipes in this section are designed to be made in combination with each other so you can end up with a wide variety of flavours on your plates. We tend to use our fingers for these informal pick and mix sessions and they always end up being great fun.

The section I found the most fun to write was Party Foods. I think the children enjoyed it most too as I was testing the recipes to make sure they would work when I wrote them down! I've tried to include ones that have worked well at my children's parties. Most of them are very quick and easy to make and will help you cut as many corners as possible. There is always so much to think about when you have to organize a children's party that I find every extra minute counts.

Above everything else, I really hope you enjoy using this book. From being a complete novice I've come to love cooking for my family – yes, even for Gordon! I also like to know that the children are getting all the nutrients they need. (I've included a chart with basic nutritional information at the back of the book as I always find them handy.) When I was little it was such a comfort coming home to my mum's cooking. I hope that my children and yours will grow up with the same feelings of love, comfort and satisfaction around food.

breakfast

The most important meal of the day!

Weekday breakfasts are tough ones. Like most people with young children, my house is always completely chaotic between 7 and 8 a.m. on a weekday. The children are all still fast asleep at 7 and have to be literally dragged out of their nice warm beds. Then we have one hour to get dressed, eat, clean teeth, wash faces, do several sets of plaits/bunches/ponytails, persuade my son to introduce his hair to a hairbrush and get out the door. I also have to make sure the beds are made and curtains open if it is a work day, as I don't want to come home to a mess in the evening. They do this themselves, but often need a reminder (or two or three!) – a little treat is always a good incentive!

school-rush smoothies

Smoothies are the most fantastic way of making sure that even a reluctant eater starts the day with a good percentage of their recommended daily intake of fresh fruit inside them. There are no hard-and-fast rules about what makes a good smoothie (although you will obviously need a liquidizer), but the ones I've included here always seem to go down well with my lot.

These are the combinations of fruit I often use, but you can vary the quantities according to your needs (and the contents of your fruit bowl).

Mango mania
1 mango
1 banana (preferably ripe)
orange juice

Berry blast
1 cup frozen berries
1 mango
orange juice

Green monkey
4 kiwis
1 banana (preferably ripe)
apple juice

1 Wash, peel and roughly chop the fruit.

2 Put into a blender and pour over enough juice to cover the fruit.

3 Blend until smooth. Enjoy!

Tips

- You can of course make your own fresh orange or apple juice, but I always 'cheat' by using a good-quality fresh fruit juice as a base. It's much easier and quicker.

- I find it incredibly useful to keep a bag of frozen berries in the freezer just for making smoothies.

fruit salad with oats and warm yoghurt

This is one of those breakfasts that is a bit fiddly, but in spite of this I try to prepare it once a week because the children love it, it is incredibly healthy, and my being lazy is a terrible excuse!

4 tbsp oat flakes
4 tbsp blueberries
4 tbsp raspberries
2 tbsp water
golden caster sugar
4 round tbsp natural organic
    yoghurt
4 tsp runny honey
    (1 tsp per portion)

Serves: 4 children
Prep time: 15 minutes
Cooking time: 5 minutes

1 Lightly toast the oat flakes in a small frying pan until golden brown. Take care not to burn them. Take off the heat and remove a few oat flakes and put aside. Meanwhile, place the blueberries and raspberries into a small saucepan, add water and a sprinkle of golden caster sugar and heat gently, stirring occasionally.

2 Add the yoghurt to the pan of toasted oat flakes and gently stir through.

3 When the fruit is nicely warm, serve the yoghurt and oatmeal into a small bowl, spoon on the fruit, drizzle over the honey and sprinkle over the reserved oat flakes.

Tips

- This is really tasty with banana, and a good way to use up any over-ripe ones laying in the bottom of the fruit bowl. Simply slice them into the yoghurt when it is in the frying pan.

- To serve this as a dessert you can simply leave out the oat flakes and crumble digestive or ginger nut biscuits into the yoghurt and add fruit.

- You can also toast some flaked almonds with the oats.

I measure the ingredients in spoons – it's too early in the morning for weighing!

wholemeal pancakes with caramelized apples

This is a delicious sweet treat for breakfast. I mix the wholemeal flour with some plain white flour, as using just wholemeal flour makes the pancakes too heavy.

75g/3oz plain flour
25g/1oz wholemeal flour
250ml/9fl oz semi-skimmed milk
2 eggs
3 Bramley apples
50g/2oz butter
½ tsp cinnamon
1 tbsp soft brown sugar

Serves: 4 children
(makes about 8 pancakes)
Prep time: 10 minutes
Cooking time: 10 minutes

1 Start by putting the flours, milk and eggs in the liquidizer and blitzing for about 2 minutes.

2 Peel and core the apples and slice quite thinly. Heat half the butter in a frying pan and add the cinnamon. Let it bubble for a minute before adding the sliced apples. Sprinkle over the sugar and very carefully turn the apples over so that they are coated in the buttery syrup. Turn the heat down and allow to cook gently. Keep an eye on them while you are cooking the pancakes and turn them over from time-to-time to allow them to cook evenly.

3 While the apples are happily cooking away, melt the rest of the butter in another frying pan and start frying the pancakes. The first pancake always seems to be a disaster, so I usually eat it myself. Pile the pancakes on a plate beside you until you have made them all.

4 Divide the apple mixture between the pancakes and roll up. Drizzle a little maple syrup over each one to guarantee a good day ahead!

Tip

- It's a good idea to make the batter the night before and leave in the fridge until the morning. As well as saving time, it improves the batter by allowing it to rest.

porridge with blueberries

I love sending the children off to school with a tummy full of porridge - you know they will have enough in there to last until lunchtime with great energy! If I am going running I know it helps my energy levels.

100g/4oz porridge oats
300ml/10½fl oz water
600ml/1 pint whole milk
150g/6oz blueberries
soft brown sugar or maple syrup

Serves: 4 children
Prep time: 5 minutes
Cooking time: 10 minutes

1 If I am making this for breakfast the next day, I always try to remember to put the oats and water in a saucepan the night before and leave it with the lid on overnight. It just reduces the cooking time, which is always a good thing when I'm trying to get everyone to school on time.

2 Pour the milk onto the oats and water and gently bring to the boil, stirring all the time.

3 Turn the heat down and simmer for about 7 minutes, until the porridge is thick and creamy.

4 Divide between four bowls, sprinkle with blueberries and a little maple syrup or sugar.

fruit gratin

Although this might seem a slightly odd choice for breakfast, it is very quick to make, especially if you make the batter the night before and leave it in the fridge. You can then simply pour the batter into the dish, pop in the fruit and put it in the oven to cook while you dress the children and yourself!

The aim of this dish is that the fruit should be surrounded by a soft, only just set, cake. It's almost like having Yorkshire pudding with jam on top! You need to serve it straight from the oven, otherwise it will continue to cook and become hard and stodgy.

butter to grease the dish
6 plums/apricots/nectarines
425ml/15fl oz milk
3 eggs
75g/3oz plain flour
50g/2oz caster sugar
50g/2oz ground almonds
1 tsp good-quality vanilla extract
seeds from vanilla pod (optional)

Serves: 6
Prep time: 10 minutes
Cooking time: 20–25 minutes

1 Preheat the oven to 200°C/400°F/GM6

2 Grease the dish and put to one side.

3 Slice the soft fruit in half and remove the stones.

4 Put the milk, eggs, flour, sugar, almonds and vanilla into the liquidizer and blitz for about 2 minutes.

5 Pour the liquid into the prepared dish and then gently arrange the fruit, cut-side down, so that all you see is the softly rounded fruit peeking out from the batter.

6 Place in the oven and cook for about 20 minutes.

7 Serve immediately.

boiled eggs with cheesy fingers

My children think this is the ultimate treat for breakfast - again, it's more of a weekend breakfast, as it takes too much thinking about for a weekday morning ...

4 large organic free range eggs
4 slices wholemeal bread
100g/4oz mature cheddar cheese,
   grated

Serves: 4
Prep time: 5 minutes
Cooking time: 7 minutes

1   Preheat the grill on high.

2   Bring to the boil a large deep saucepan of water and carefully add the eggs. Remember to set the timer for 5 minutes – I easily get distracted so always work by my timer! Toast the wholemeal bread and cover with the cheddar. Place under the grill until the cheese is bubbling.

3   Remove the eggs from the pan, place in a sieve and run under the cold tap to stop over-cooking – eggs that are too hard-boiled are not the same!

4   Crack the top of the egg and remove the shell on the top third. Place into an egg cup and slice off the white to reveal a lovely runny yolk.

5   Cut the cheesy toast into soldiers and dip into the yolk! Serve.

Tip

• If you keep your eggs in the fridge, allow them to reach room temperature before boiling – this helps prevent them cracking as they boil.

It's only when you taste boiled eggs that you remember how good they are.

field mushrooms on toast

This may sound like a very grown-up breakfast for children, but I find if I am eating it my children are always hanging around for a taste.

1 loaf ciabatta
4 tbsp olive oil
400g/14oz portabellini or other
    large mushrooms
20g/¾oz bunch of basil
25g/1oz parmesan, finely grated

1 Cut the ciabatta in half vertically and again horizontally. Drizzle with a bit of the olive oil and place on a baking sheet.

2 Cut mushrooms into thick slices.

3 Heat the remaining olive oil in a large saucepan until shimmering, then throw in the mushrooms.

4 Cook on a fairly high heat, stirring regularly until the mushrooms start to release their natural liquid.

5 Turn off the heat, add a few torn basil leaves and put the lid on. Leave to infuse while you grill the ciabatta on a fairly high heat for about 5 minutes until it is just browning and going crunchy.

6 As soon as the bread is ready, place on plates, divide the mushrooms between them and sprinkle with the remaining basil leaves and parmesan.

Serves: 4
Prep time: 10 minutes
Cooking time: 10 minutes

Tip

● Dice two or three really ripe, sweet vine tomatoes and sprinkle on top.

poached eggs on wholemeal toast

285ml/½ pint water
4 medium eggs
   (free-range/organic if possible)
4 slices wholemeal toast
butter

Serves: 4 children
Prep time: 10 minutes
Cooking time: 5 minutes

1 Put the water into a small pan and bring to the boil. Crack one egg into a cup. Using a spoon, stir the water in the pan very quickly to create a 'whirlpool'. Slide the egg into the water then simmer for 3 minutes until the egg is firmly set. Remove with a slotted spoon.

2 Repeat with the remaining eggs.

3 Serve the poached eggs on hot buttered toast.

Tips

- Fantastic served with a slice of ham underneath the egg, or grated cheddar cheese on top.

- It is even easier to make this if you buy little egg poachers that clip onto the side of a saucepan.

muesli

Muesli can contain many different dried fruits and nuts, but this combination is the one we like best.

300g/10oz rolled oats
35g/1½oz dried banana chips
35g/1½oz dried coconut flakes
600ml/1 pint fresh orange
 (or apple) juice
400ml/⅔pint natural yoghurt
100g/4oz raisins
100g/4oz dried cranberries
100g/4oz dried apricots cut into
 small chunks
125ml/¼pint runny honey
300ml/½ pint whole milk
50g lightly toasted flaked
 almonds

1 Mix together the oats, banana chips and coconut flakes with the juice and yoghurt in a mixing bowl. Cover with clingfilm and leave overnight in the fridge.

2 Add all the dried fruit, honey and milk into the oat mixture and stir through.

3 Just before serving sprinkle over the toasted flaked almonds.

Serves: 4–6
Prep time: 15 minutes
Cooking time: soak overnight to allow oats to swell and soften

Tips

- This is delicious served with a warm fruit sauce. Simply place a handful of red berries (blueberries and raspberries are my favourites) into a small pan with a teaspoon of caster sugar and gently heat until they start to bleed and soften. Spoon onto the top.

- Apple is also delicious simply sliced or grated on the top.

homemade baked beans

This is a delicious alternative to the traditional tinned varieties! I would not dare compare - I am a huge fan myself - but I love this recipe and find that when I have the time it is great to do a couple of batches at once. I use what I need and then freeze what's left.

450g/1lb dried haricot beans
3 medium onions
4 cloves garlic
3 tbsp olive oil
2 level tsp paprika
½ tsp ground cloves
3 heaped tbsp tomato ketchup
250ml/9fl oz passata
300ml/10½fl oz water
1 tbsp Worcestershire sauce
salt
1 rounded tsp soft brown sugar

1 The night before, put the beans in a large bowl and cover well with water. Leave them to soak overnight.

2 The following morning, drain and rinse the beans. Put them in the casserole, cover with water and simmer on the hob for 1 hour.

3 Preheat the oven to 150°C/300°F/GM2.

4 While the beans are simmering, make the sauce. Start by frying the onions and garlic in the olive oil on a gentle heat. When the onions are soft and golden, sprinkle in the paprika and ground cloves and stir for about 1 minute. Then stir in the ketchup and mix well. Gently add the passata and water and bring to the boil. Simmer for about 10 minutes before liquidizing until smooth.

5 Once the beans are cooked, drain, return to the casserole and pour over the tomato sauce. Add Worcestershire sauce, salt and sugar. Stir well and bring to the boil. Put the lid on and place in the oven. Bake for 1 hour.

6 After an hour, check the beans and, if necessary (which it always seems to be!) add some more boiling water. Cook for another hour. Before serving, check whether the beans need more liquid, and if you think they do, stir in some more boiling water.

Serves: 6–8
Prep time: 15 minutes
Cooking time: 3 hours
(plus overnight soaking of beans)

full english

Every one has their own idea of the perfect full English breakfast - this is my version. (Strictly for weekends or school holidays as this is far too messy for weekdays!)

2 tbsp olive oil
12 chipolata sausages
12 rashers of bacon
   (I love maple bacon)
1 tin baked beans (or your own
   if you have any made!)
6 large field mushrooms
6 plum tomatoes
pepper to taste
6 large free-range (and if possible
   organic) eggs
fresh wholemeal bread
margarine

1 One of the hardest things with cooked breakfast is timing everything together and keeping it all warm! To help with this, preheat the oven to 130°C/250°F/GM½ and put in your serving plates and a large platter.

2 Heat the olive oil in a large frying pan and add the chipolatas, cooking slowly for about 10 minutes until they start to spit. Add the bacon and cook until it begins to crisp. The sausages should now be nice and brown. Pop these into the oven onto the large platter to keep warm.

3 Place the baked beans in a small saucepan and heat gently. Do not allow to overheat.

4 Lower the heat in the frying pan and add the mushrooms and tomatoes. Season these with some pepper and gently fry for approximately 5 minutes.

5 Meanwhile in a separate frying pan heat a little oil and crack the eggs carefully into it. Cook until the white is completely set and firm.

6 Toast the wholemeal bread and spread with margarine.

7 Serve!

Serves: 6
Prep time: 5–10 minutes
Cooking time: 30 minutes

herring roe on toast

This was a dish I used to enjoy as a child - my mum always used to do it for my grandmother who lived with us. I remember Mum being surprised that I loved it so much, but that is often the way - children like the most unlikely foods at times, and we miss that because we never give them different things to try. This became my favourite Saturday morning breakfast. Incredibly easy and quick to make.

knob of butter
300g/12oz soft herring roe
couple of twists of black pepper
  to taste
1 lemon (cut into quarters
  lengthways)
4 slices wholemeal toast

Serves: 4 children
Prep time: 5 minutes
Cooking time: 5 minutes

1 Simply melt the butter in a medium-sized frying pan.

2 Put in the herring roe and sauté gently, until the roe is firm. This takes approximately 2–3 minutes. Twist in the black pepper and serve onto hot buttered toast.

3 Squeeze over the lemon and serve!

Tip

- A sprinkling of chives adds great flavour.

smoked haddock kedgeree

25g/1oz butter
1 tsp ground coriander
1 tsp ground cumin
¼ tsp turmeric
250g/8oz basmati rice
450ml/16fl oz water
pinch Maldon sea salt
2 free-range eggs
450g/1lb smoked haddock fillet
125ml/4½fl oz milk
125ml/4½fl oz double cream
2 spring onions, finely chopped
2 tbsp coriander, chopped

Serves: 4 hungry children
Prep time: 10 minutes
Cooking time: 20 minutes

1 Melt the butter in a medium saucepan, then add the spices and the rice. Cook this for approximately 2 minutes. Add the water and salt. Bring this to the boil and simmer for 10 minutes.

2 Place the eggs into a saucepan of boiling water and boil for 6 minutes, so they are not too runny in the centre, but not fully hard – you want them to have a lovely bright yellow yolk that is almost creamy in texture.

3 Meanwhile, put the haddock in a saucepan with the milk and cream and heat to a simmer. When simmering, cover and allow to cook for approximately 5 minutes.

4 When the eggs are ready, run them under a cold tap to stop them overcooking, then peel and put aside till ready to serve. Take out the haddock, remove the skin and flake the fish, carefully removing any bones. Put the flakes back into the milk and cream.

5 Stir the rice and add to the haddock, sprinkle in the spring onions, chop the eggs and add to the dish, gently stirring through. Sprinkle the coriander over the top and serve.

Tip

● This is also delicious if you add fresh peas.

lunch bites

Food on the go doesn't have to be basic or boring. The challenge is to think of ways of incorporating healthy options. The only catch is, you want ideas which can be made the night before, or put together quickly, as we all need to rush out of the door on a weekday morning and none of us has time to fiddle around. Even being able to have sandwich fillings ready, or salads to spoon into containers, is a start.

The other important aspect to consider is choosing things that will satisfy – you don't want your children to end up picking up a bag of crisps or a chocolate bar because lunch left them feeling hungry. You want to have energy and feel like you have had something healthy and filling – and a little different from the ordinary cheese sandwich.

ham and cheese muffins

Very basic, very tasty!

300g/10½oz self-raising flour
½ tsp mustard powder
½ tsp paprika
75g/3oz butter
6 slices honey roast ham,
    chopped into 1-cm pieces
185g/6½oz mature cheddar cheese,
    grated
1 egg, beaten
250ml/9fl oz milk
6 tbsp finely grated parmesan
    (to sprinkle on the top)

Makes: 12 muffins
Prep time: 15 minutes
Cooking time: 20 minutes

1 Preheat oven to 190°C/375°F/GM5.

2 Lightly grease a 12-hole muffin tin
   (alternatively, use muffin cases in the holes
   – I prefer this).

3 Sieve the flour, mustard powder and paprika
   into a large mixing bowl. Rub in the butter
   until this resembles breadcrumbs. Add the
   ham and cheese, then stir in the egg and
   milk.

4 Spoon equal amounts of the mix into the
   12 muffin cases and sprinkle a little parmesan
   on top of each.

5 Bake for 20 minutes.

6 Remove to a wire cooling rack.

Tip

● It's a good idea to make these in bulk and them freeze the muffins individually. You can then
  take them out of the freezer the night before.

danish pastry pizzas

These pizzas are just like savoury Danish pastries - hence the name! I like to make a batch and freeze them for packed lunches.

300g/10½oz strong white flour
½ tsp fast-acting/easy-bake yeast
½ tsp caster sugar
1 tsp salt
1 tbsp olive oil
200ml/7fl oz tepid water
4 tbsp passata
100g/4oz thinly sliced ham or
    Parma ham
1 tsp dried oregano
125g/5oz grated mozzarella
salt and pepper

Makes: 12
Prep time: 20 minutes
(but best to leave the dough
to rise for 40 minutes)
Cooking time: 25 minutes

1 Preheat oven to 180°C/350°F/GM4.

2 I have an electric food mixer, so tend to make my dough using that. It is no easier using the mixer, however, it just saves a bit of time and allows you to be doing something else while the mixer works away. Having said that, kneading dough has to be one of the most satisfying and pleasing things to do and, if the house is quiet and there's nobody asking me to do a hundred other things, it really is very relaxing!

3 To make the dough, put the flour, yeast, sugar and salt in a large mixing bowl. If using a mixer, put all the wet ingredients in as well (the oil and water) and turn on the machine. If making by hand, make a well in the middle and pour in the oil and water. Using a spoon to begin with, stir the liquid around and as the flour slowly collapses into the liquid, mix into a dough. Once you have a lump of dough, start using your hands. Bring the dough onto a well-floured work surface and begin kneading. Using the heel of your hands, pull the dough towards you before pushing back into the main mound of mixture. Alternate hands, and before long you will have a lovely, soothing rhythm going that will be doing no end of good to the muscle tone in your upper arms!

4 After 5 minutes, place the dough into a clean mixing bowl and leave in a warm place to rise for 40 minutes.

5   After the 40 minutes is up, the dough should have nearly doubled in size. Take out of the bowl and knead again for a minute or so before pulling the dough into a rectangular shape, roughly 40cm x 25cm, on a large chopping board.

6   Spoon the passata over the pizza dough and spread evenly around. Sprinkle evenly with the ham, dried oregano, mozzarella and seasoning.

7   Turn the pizza so that the longest side of the rectangle is in front of you. Very gingerly, start rolling the pizza up, just like a swiss roll.

8   Cut into 12 pieces, approximately 1cm thick and carefully put on a baking sheet, lined with baking parchment, cut side up.

9   Bake for 25 minutes.

coleslaw crunch

This is great served in a little Tupperware tub to accompany a simple sandwich or muffin - and a good way to approach Brussels sprouts ... Love them or hate them.

4 Brussels sprouts, finely
   shredded
4 grated carrots
1 grated apple
1 stick celery, finely sliced
2 tbsp raisins
8 seedless white grapes, cut into
   quarters
½ lemon, juice
2 tbsp mayonnaise (some prefer
   2 tbsp salad cream)

Makes: 4 portions
Prep time: 20 minutes

1 Finely shred the Brussels sprouts into a mixing bowl, add the carrots, apple and the celery, the raisins and the grapes. Squeeze over the lemon juice and stir through the mayonnaise.

2 Divide into 4 Tupperware containers.

salami and rice salad medley

Incredibly easy to put together and a really delicious, healthy and colourful salad. The creamy dressing coats the rice and salami beautifully - deceptively filling!

200g/8oz brown rice, cooked to
   instructions on packet
drizzle of olive oil
200g/8oz red kidney beans,
   cooked
2 sticks celery, chopped
6 spring onions, finely chopped
1 red pepper, deseeded and finely
   chopped
340g/12oz tin of sweetcorn
200g/8oz salami cut into chunks

For the dressing
5 tbsp olive oil
4 tbsp balsamic vinegar
2 tbsp crème fraîche

Serves: 4 good-sized portions
(more if part of a selection)
Prep time: 15 minutes
Cooking time: 10–12 minutes
(just the rice-cooking time)

1 When the rice is cooked, drain into a sieve and run under the cold tap. Drizzle through the olive oil and stir through.

2 Place in a large mixing bowl with the other ingredients, mix together the dressing and stir through, mixing everything and ensuring an even coating of dressing.

3 Serve in little Tupperware containers as part of a lunch box.

golden puff pastries

200g/8oz steak mince
2 tbsp olive oil
1 medium onion, finely chopped
150g/6oz carrots, diced
100g/4oz parsnips, diced
2 level tbsp plain flour
250ml/9fl oz water with half of a
    quality beef stock cube
75g/3oz frozen peas
black pepper to taste
500-g/1-lb pack puff pastry
1 egg, beaten

Makes: 15
Prep time: 10 minutes
Cooking time: 1 hour

1 Preheat oven to 180°C/350°F/GM4.

2 Start by frying the mince in the olive oil until browned. Break it down with a wooden spoon to make sure there are no lumps.

3 Add the onion, carrots and parsnips and continue to cook for 5 minutes.

4 Sprinkle over the flour and stir well until completely mixed together. Add the water and stock cube and keep stirring until it comes to the boil. Reduce heat and simmer very gently for about 40 minutes until liquid has reduced and there is only a little thick gravy left.

5 Add the frozen peas and mix in. Remove from the heat.

6 Carefully roll out the puff pastry until it is about 3mm thick.

7 Using a saucer as a template, cut around the outside with a sharp knife until you have as many small circles as you can make.

8 Take a dessertspoon and put one spoonful of the mince mixture in the middle of each pastry disk. Using your fingertip, edge the pastry with a little water and fold the pastry in half over the top of the filling. Push down the edges of the semi-circle with your fingers to seal.

9 Using a pastry brush, carefully brush each pasty with the beaten egg.

10 Place on a baking tray covered with baking parchment and bake for 15 minutes until golden brown.

11 Allow to cool before wrapping individually and freezing in a plastic box.

stuffed potato cakes

I discovered these by chance. I tried them when Gordon and I were in the Maldives and had them as a mezze. I found that the children enjoyed them even when they were cold - if they had a minty yoghurt dip. They are the perfect nutritious addition to any lunchbox!

For the potato outsides
700g/1lb 7oz potatoes, with skins on
1½ tbsp plain flour
salt

For the filling
50g/2oz pine nuts
1 red onion, finely chopped
2 tbsp olive oil
25g/1oz butter
1 tsp ground cinnamon
1 tsp grated nutmeg
3 cloves
200g/7oz minced lamb
1 tbsp tomato purée
handful of spinach
5 dried apricots, finely chopped
  (or 2tbsp cranberries)
3 tbsp chopped flat leaf parsley
2 tbsp Worcestershire sauce
salt and pepper

For the dip
2 tbsp fresh mint
8 tbsp crème fraîche
1 lemon, juice

Makes: 12 cakes
Prep/cooking time: 45 minutes

1 For the dip, simply chop the mint and stir into the crème fraîche with the lemon juice.

2 Boil the potatoes whole and with their skins in lightly salted water until just cooked — be careful not to overcook, they should simmer, not boil furiously, and you should just be able to pierce with the tip of a knife. Drain well, and when cool enough to handle, peel.

3 Mash the potatoes and sprinkle over the flour, mixing in throughout. Add a little salt and mould into a dough. Place this aside now while you make the filling.

4 Lightly toast the pine nuts in a small pan until golden. Gently fry the onion in another pan with the olive oil and butter. Add the cinnamon, nutmeg and cloves and allow this to form a paste with the onions.

5 Add the lamb mince and stir until it begins to brown. Allow to brown a little more than usual, then add the tomato purée, spinach, pine nuts, dried apricots (or cranberries) and the parsley, Worcestershire sauce and a little seasoning. Stir together and allow to continue frying gently for a couple of minutes until the spinach has wilted, then put aside to cool.

6 Break the potato dough into 12 small balls and sprinkle a little flour over your hands and your work surface. Flatten one of the pieces into a circle shape using the palm of your hand. Put approximately 2 tablespoons of the lamb mince mix into the centre, then bring up the edges to enclose and mould into a nice neat cake shape. Knead together any cracks with your hands and generally make into a smooth surface with floury hands. Each cake should be about 2cm thick and 5cm wide. Repeat this with the other dough balls, keeping flour on the surface and your hands.

7 Using a large and fairly deep frying pan, heat up 3–4mm of oil until it is just lightly smoking. Put the potato cakes in one by one, taking care not to splash the oil or damage the cakes. Leave them to fry until golden in colour then turn carefully.

8 Once they are golden all over, place onto kitchen roll to absorb excess oil.

Tip

- Best eaten warm, but my kids enjoy them when they are cold, especially with the dip! A great addition to any lunch box!

sandwich fillers

All these fillers keep well if you make them the night before.

salmon and cream cheese with lemon

100g/4oz salmon fillet, cooked
100g/4oz smoked salmon
   trimmings
200g/8oz cream cheese
1 lemon, juiced
pepper

1 Put all the ingredients in the bowl of a food processor and blitz until smooth.

Prep time: 10 minutes
Makes: 2 rounds of sandwiches

coronation chicken

200g/8oz cooked chicken
   (preferably the leftovers from
   a roast chicken)
1 tbsp mild curry paste
1 tbsp mayonnaise
½ lemon, juiced
salt and pepper

1 Cut the chicken into small, child-friendly pieces. In a small saucepan gently cook the curry paste for about 5 minutes, stirring all the time. Allow to cool completely.

2 In a bowl combine the chicken, mayonnaise, cooled curry paste and lemon juice. Check seasoning.

Prep time: 10 minutes
Makes: 2 rounds of sandwiches

smoked mackerel and cream cheese

250g/10oz smoked mackerel
   fillets, skin and bones removed
2 tsp horseradish
100g/4oz cream cheese
pepper

1 Put all ingredients in the mixer and pulse until mixed together but maintaining an interesting texture.

Prep time: 10 minutes
Makes: 2 rounds of sandwiches

easy sausage rolls

200g/8oz sausage meat
25g/1oz onion, finely chopped
1 tsp dried sage
salt and pepper
½ x 500g/1lb pack puff pastry
1 tbsp flour for dusting
1 tsp mustard powder
1 tbsp sesame seeds
1 egg, beaten

1 Preheat oven to 180°C/350°F/GM4.

2 Combine the sausage meat, onion, sage, salt and pepper.

3 Roll out the pastry into a rectangle that is about 3mm thick. Cut in half lengthwise. Lightly dust the inside of the pastry with flour, adding the mustard powder for a little kick! Sprinkle over the sesame seeds.

4 Using wet hands, divide the sausage meat into two equal portions. Take each portion and roll into two long sausages. Place one down the centre of each pastry strip.

5 Dampen one long edge of each pastry length and bring the pastry over the sausage mixture, pressing the edges together and then carefully rolling the entire sausage until the join is underneath the roll.

6 Brush with the beaten egg and cut into 3cm lengths.

7 Place on a baking sheet lined with baking parchment and carefully stab each sausage roll a couple of times with the point of a sharp knife.

8 Bake for about 20–25 minutes or until golden.

9 Allow to cool before wrapping individually and freezing in a plastic box.

Makes: 12
Prep time: 20 minutes
Cooking time: 20–25 minutes

omelette

This chive omelette served with a tangy tomato salad is a perfect lunch bite for one! The tomato salad is very simple - the acidic vinaigrette cuts beautifully through the richness of the omelette.

2–3 very fresh eggs
  (depending on hunger level!)
2 tbsp freshly chopped chives
salt and pepper
4 ripe tomatoes
½ tsp grapeseed oil and a similar
  quantity of butter

For the vinaigrette
4 tbsp light olive oil
2 tbsp white wine vinegar
salt and pepper

Serves: 1
Prep time: ½ hour to infuse
Cooking time: 10 minutes

1 Crack the eggs into a bowl, add the chives, salt and pepper and gently mix together with a fork. Leave for about half an hour, if you can, to allow the flavours to infuse.

2 While the egg and chives are doing their thing, slice the tomatoes and arrange on a plate. Whisk together the vinaigrette ingredients and pour over. Let the flavours develop while you make the omelette.

3 Heat the pan over a medium heat for about a minute before adding the oil and then the butter (this will stop the butter burning). Swirl the oil and butter around the pan, making sure the surface is evenly coated.

4 Turn up the heat to the highest setting and, as soon as the butter starts to foam, pour in the eggs. Gently rotate the pan to make sure the eggs evenly coat the surface of the pan.

5 After about 5 seconds, tilt the pan to an angle of about 45 degrees. Using a flat spatula, pull it up from the edge of the pan to the centre, allowing the liquid egg to fill the empty space. Keep doing this until there is only a small amount of liquid left on the surface.

6 With the help of the spatula, flip one side of the omelette over to the centre. Take the pan to a warm plate and tip the omelette onto it, folding it over as you do so.

7 Serve immediately with the tomato salad.

chocolate chip cookies

An old favourite! These are great in a lunch box - often I slip these in for a Friday treat. If the children smell these cooking at home they always hang around - no doubt about it, these are at their best when they are cooling and the chocolate is all gooey!

300g/12oz good-quality milk
   chocolate
200g/8oz softened unsalted butter
100g/4oz caster sugar
150g/6oz soft light brown sugar
2 eggs, beaten
300g/12oz plain flour
1 tsp vanilla essence
1 tsp bicarbonate of soda

Makes: 40 cookies
Prep time: 15 minutes
Cooking time: 10–15 minutes

1 Preheat oven to 180°C/350°F/GM4.

2 Lightly grease a baking sheet.

3 Firstly, break the chocolate into small chunks, then place into a plastic bag and hammer with a rolling pin to make smaller. Watch your fingers!

4 Beat together the butter and the sugars in a large mixing bowl until light in colour and smooth. Beat in the eggs, stirring through. Add the flour, vanilla essence and bicarbonate of soda, and stir in the chocolate chunks.

5 Spoon mounds of the mixture onto your greased baking sheet, ensuring you leave space around each mound, as they will spread.

6 Bake for 10–15 minutes until golden brown. They will continue to set while cooling, so be careful not to over cook. Once removed from the oven allow 10 minutes to set then place onto a wire cooling rack.

oatmeal and cranberry crunch biscuits

100g/4oz wholemeal flour
100g/4oz plain flour
75g/3oz oatmeal
75g/3oz bran
125g/5oz Muscovado sugar
½ tsp ground ginger
100g/4oz unsalted butter
150ml/¼ pint cold water
100g/4oz dried cranberries

Makes: 48 biscuits
Prep time: 15 minutes
Cooking time: 20–25 minutes

1 Preheat oven to 180°C/350°F/GM4.

2 Put all the dry ingredients except the cranberries into a large mixing bowl and mix well. Rub in the butter until the mix resembles breadcrumbs, then add the water and the cranberries and mix into a dough.

3 Lightly flour your work surface and roll out the dough to approximately 1cm thickness. Cut out with a round cookie cutter approximately 6cm in diameter.

4 Place the crunchies onto a lightly greased baking tray and bake for 20–25 minutes.

5 When ready, remove from the baking tray immediately with a flat slice and leave to cool on a wire rack – this just ensures the bottoms do not overcook.

Tips

- These are great for a mid-morning snack.
- You can substitute any dried fruit for the cranberries.

chocolate nut temptations

You know you are full and that you probably shouldn't, but somehow you find the room ...

50g/2oz whole shelled hazelnuts
25g/1oz almonds
25g/1oz shelled pistachio nuts
400g/15oz milk chocolate
50g/2oz raisins

1 Peel any brown skin off the hazelnuts and almonds, and break in half. If you prefer smaller pieces, crush them up. Toast along with the pistachios in a shallow frying pan – do not use oil. This only takes 5–6 minutes.

2 Meanwhile, break the milk chocolate into small chunks and melt in a small bowl over a pan of simmering water. When melted, pour the chocolate into the bottom of a shallow baking tray lined with baking parchment. Sprinkle the nuts and raisins onto the top of this and gently shake the tray to allow them to slightly sink into the chocolate.

3 Place the tray into the fridge and leave to harden. This takes at least 2½ hours, but is best if left overnight.

Serves: 6, as a snack
Prep time: 10 minutes
Setting time: 2½ hours
(or make the night before)

4 When it is set and you are ready to indulge, remove from the fridge and gently peel the parchment off the back of the chocolate. Break into pieces and serve!

Tip

● Follow this recipe in exactly the same way, but use white chocolate and quantities of dried cranberries, almonds and apricots (or any dried fruit you desire). Remember, only toast the nuts, not the fruit!

date and hazelnut fingers

Delicious and so easy to make!

2 eggs
175g/6oz Muscovado sugar
75g/3oz wholemeal self-raising
　　flour
50g/2oz bran cereal
50g/2oz crushed hazelnuts
100g/4oz stoned dates, chopped

Makes: 12 fingers
Prep time: 10 minutes
Cooking time: 25–30 minutes

1　Preheat oven to 180°C/350°F/GM4.

2　First, line and lightly grease a baking tin 11 x 7"
　　(28 x 18cm).

3　Put the eggs and sugar into a large mixing
　　bowl and whisk together until light and fluffy.

4　Stir in the remaining ingredients and mix
　　together well. Pour the mixture into the lined
　　baking tin and smooth evenly.

5　Bake in the oven for 25–30 minutes.

6　When cooked, remove from the oven and
　　leave to cool in the tin.

7　Cut into finger slices and serve!

Tip

● Keep in an air-tight container if not eating straight away.

tea-time treats

I think it would be terribly unrealistic to say that children should never have snacks – I love them, and certainly as a child it was one of the comforts that I needed!

Quite often children need a little pick-me-up when they finish school. It is a little too long to wait until supper is ready, yet lunch was hours ago. A small snack is a very welcome treat, but you want to give a little more than just a packet of sweets or a chocolate bar, not least because these will just not satisfy.

Not all of the recipes in this section are the healthiest option, but in moderation and given as a snack at the right time they certainly will not hurt. They give the right kind of energy pick-up and help to wean children off the typical packet of crisps or sticky sweets. I also feel a sense of relief knowing exactly what is in the snacks I'm giving my children.

These will all last a couple of days if stored correctly in an air-tight container, and the children can even help you make many of them – you have to let them make a mess sometimes!

banana and apple loaf

A slice of this loaf is a very satisfying treat - the banana makes it a substantial snack and a real energy boost.

150g/5oz light Muscovado sugar
85g/3¼oz unsalted butter, softened
2 large free-range eggs, beaten
4 medium-sized ripe bananas, mashed
1 apple, grated
250g/8oz self-raising flour
¼ tsp freshly grated nutmeg
¼ tsp cinnamon
pinch of salt

Makes: a small loaf of approximately 15 slices
Prep time: 15 minutes
Cooking time: 45 minutes

1 Preheat oven to 180°C/350°F/GM4. Grease and line a 900g/2lb loaf tin.

2 Cream together the sugar, butter and eggs.

3 Stir in the mashed bananas and apple and sieve in the flour, nutmeg, cinnamon and salt.

4 Once well mixed, tip into the loaf tin and bake for 40–45 minutes.

5 Remove to a wire rack and cool in the tin for 20–30 minutes. Remove from the tin onto the rack and finish cooling completely before slicing.

6 Serve.

Tip

- Also great to have a slice for breakfast!

chocolate crunch brownies

Naughty but nice is the only way to describe these! Definitely one to keep for special occasions.

250g/8oz unsalted butter
425g/14oz golden caster sugar
4 large free-range eggs, beaten
65g/2½oz plain flour
40g/1½oz cocoa powder
400g/13oz plain chocolate
   (either chips or a bar broken
   into small pieces)

Makes: 24 brownies
Prep time: 20 minutes
Cooking time: 30–35 minutes

1 Preheat oven to 180°C/350°F/GM4.

2 Melt the butter in a small pan and pour into a large mixing bowl. Add the sugar and eggs, mixing well. Then add the flour and cocoa powder.

3 Add the chocolate chunks and stir through. Lightly grease the square tin and pour in the mixture.

4 Bake for 30–35 minutes.

5 Remove from the oven and cut into 2-inch squares. Using a palette knife, remove from the tin and place onto a cooling rack. This helps to stop the brownies over-cooking and becoming a little dry.

Tips

- As soon as they are cool, place into an air-tight container to maintain freshness.

- It's best to place the chocolate pieces in a bag and hit them with a rolling pin. I prefer to use a bar of plain chocolate broken into chunks, as it helps to make the brownies a little more rugged and you get a lovely chocolate surprise if you bite into a large chocolate bit!

- These do contain a lot of sugar and are obviously best kept as a treat and not a regular snack.

orange sponge fingers with lemon icing

These sponge fingers are incredibly light, and the taste of orange and lemon together gives them a really fresh kick.

For the sponge
175g/6oz unsalted butter, softened
175g/6oz golden caster sugar
3 large eggs, beaten
175g/6oz self-raising flour, sieved
2 tbsp orange juice

For the icing
200g/7oz icing sugar, sieved
2 tbsp lemon juice
1 tsp lemon zest
1 tsp water

Makes: 12 fingers
Prep time: 15 minutes
Cooking time: 20 minutes

1 Preheat oven to 180°C/350°F/GM4.

2 Mix together all the sponge ingredients. Once smooth, pour the mixture into a lined and greased 22cm x 32cm baking tin.

3 Place in the oven and bake for approximately 15–20 minutes until the sponge is lightly golden and bounces back to the touch.

4 Remove from the oven and carefully tip out of the baking tin onto a wire cooling rack. Leave to cool completely.

5 Place the sponge onto a chopping board. Slice into fingers of approximately 24cm x 8cm. Leave the fingers lined up on the board.

6 Mix together the ingredients for the icing, adding a little more water if it seems too stiff, but not too much.

7 Place the icing mix into a piping bag and drizzle artistically over the fingers!

8 Leave aside until the icing is set.

Tips

- As soon as the icing has set, put the fingers in an air-tight container to keep as fresh as possible.

- Also try lemon fingers with lime icing, or orange fingers with strawberry icing.

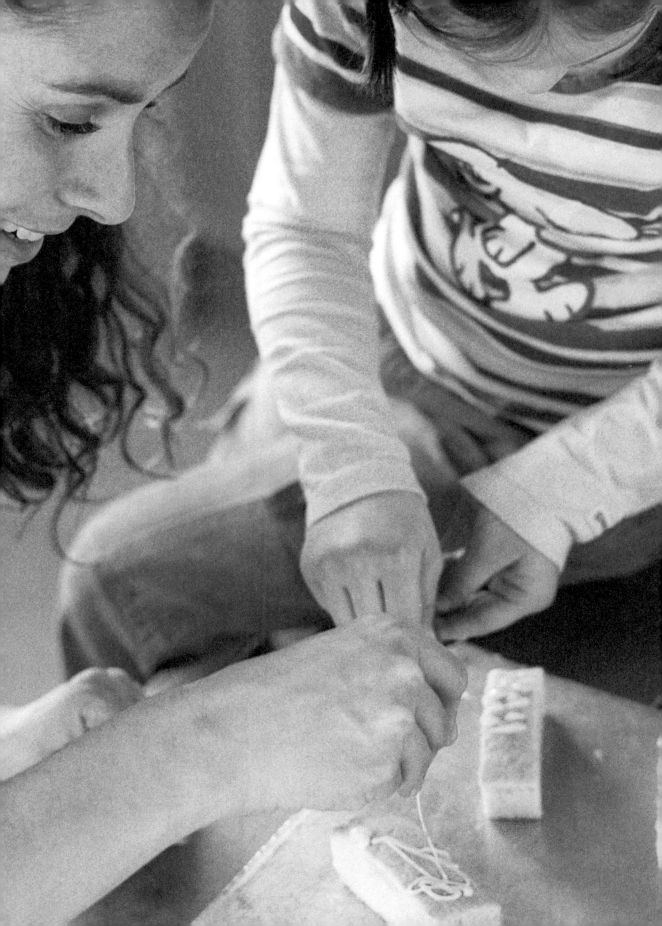

Don't be put off if your dough looks wrong, somehow it all comes right in the end and they taste fabulous!

mini jam doughnuts

After a few disasters, I have managed to adapt a recipe from Stuart Gillies at Boxwood Café. These are still a little tricky to make, so do not become disheartened if you fail on the first attempt - I promise they are well worth the effort! You will need a deep fat fryer to make these, or a deep saucepan with oil at 90-100°C, and a plastic syringe for inserting the jam.

For the dough
1 tbsp yeast
200ml/⅓ pint water
200g/7oz plain flour

And the rest
pinch of salt
120g/4oz sugar
500g/1lb flour
1 tbsp yeast
6 large egg yolks
90g/3oz softened butter
raspberry jam
    (approximately 1 tbsp
    per doughnut)
caster sugar
    (to dust the doughnuts)

Makes: 30 mini doughnuts

1 Combine the dough ingredients and let it rest.

2 Mix all the remaining ingredients (EXCEPT the butter, jam and caster sugar) into a dough and leave until it doubles in size.

3 Mix in the dough, and add 90g of softened butter. Again, let the dough rest for approximately ½ hour. Roll the dough into small (4cm diameter) balls.

4 Lower a ball of dough carefully into the hot oil. It is best to do only 2 or 3 at a time. Fry for 4–5 minutes, turning over mid way. They should be nice and golden brown when ready.

5 Remove and blot onto kitchen roll. Whilst still hot, roll in the caster sugar then leave to cool.

6 Add 2 tsp of boiling water to the raspberry jam and push them through a sieve with the back of a spoon to thin and remove the pips. The jam needs to be thin enough to be sucked into the syringe but not sloppy. You can use a piping bag with a small nozzle, but a child's medicine syringe works best as it leaves the smallest indent in the doughnut.

7 Fill the syringe with jam. Insert into the side of the doughnut and squeeze in the jam.

homemade jammy dodgers

I love these biscuits. The jam gives an energy boost and the ground almonds within the biscuit dough keep them from being too dry. A great treat to have in the cupboard.

225g/7½oz unsalted butter, diced
100g/3½oz caster sugar
200g/7oz plain flour
100g/3½oz ground almonds
150g/5oz raspberry jam, I prefer
  with seeds as it adds to the
  texture
icing sugar for dusting (optional)

Makes: 25 biscuits
Prep time: 20 minutes (but best to rest the biscuit dough for at least 5 hours)
Cooking time: 25–30 minutes

Tips

- For parties or for a change, try using different flavour jams such as apricot or strawberry – or, for a real treat, chocolate spread!

- If you're feeling particularly creative, you can save the cut-out centres and dip them in melted chocolate, once cooked, and save as snack treats.

1 Put the butter, sugar, plain flour and almonds into a mixing bowl (or food mixer). Mix all together, remove and knead into a large dough ball. Wrap in clingfilm and leave in the fridge for at least 5 hours.

2 Remove the dough and knead it until it softens enough to shape and roll. When it's ready to use, sprinkle a little plain flour over your work surface and roll out the biscuit pastry, one-third at a time. The dough should be approximately 5mm thick. Using a fluted cutter of 6cm diameter, cut out an even number of shapes. Using a palette knife, place half of these cookies onto a greased baking sheet.

3 Choose the shape of cutter you would like to use for the bit cut out of the middle – it needs to be approximately 2cm. Cut out the centre of the second batch of pastry shapes. Carefully transfer these onto a baking sheet. Place in the oven at 140°C/275°F/GM1 for approximately 30 minutes.

4 Remove the cookies from the oven and take them off the baking tray straight away onto a cooling rack (this keeps the bottoms from over-cooking). Allow to cool completely.

5 Place a blob of jam onto the centre of the 'bottom' halves of the biscuits. Be quite generous as you want the jam to show out of the edges when you put on the 'top' halves. Sieve a little icing sugar over the top.

peanut butter and raisin cookies

A great energy-boosting cookie made with fabulous crunchy peanuts and soft chewy raisins. The self-raising flour helps to keep the dough light.

200g/8oz unsalted softened butter
200g/8oz golden caster sugar
400g/15oz self-raising flour
4 tbsp milk
100g/4oz raisins
100g/4oz roasted unsalted peanuts

Makes: 24 large cookies
Prep time: 20 minutes
Cooking time: 15 minutes

1 Preheat the oven to 160°C/320°F/GM3.

2 Cream together the butter and sugar until soft. Mix in the flour, milk, raisins and peanuts and form into a large ball of dough.

3 Make small dough balls of approximately 4cm in diameter and place onto the baking tray, allowing good space around them as they will spread. Gently push down and flatten each dough ball a little so they spread to approximately 6cm flat.

4 Place into the oven and bake for approximately 15 minutes. They should be lightly golden and spring up when touched.

5 Remove from the oven and immediately place the cookies on a wire cooling rack to prevent the bottoms over-cooking.

6 Allow to cool before serving.

Tips

- Store in an air-tight container to maintain freshness.

- If you have nut allergies substitute the peanuts for white chocolate chunks. These are delicious with either raisins or dried cranberries.

fresh ginger cake

Whenever I make this cake, I always make two. They freeze so well that it seems silly not to. It is always reassuring to know that there is a homemade cake in the freezer waiting for any unexpected guests or for when I don't have time to make a snack.

150g/5oz unsalted butter
1 tsp dried cinnamon
1 tsp powdered ginger
1 tbsp black treacle
3 tbsp golden syrup
125g/4½oz soft dark sugar
1 dessertspoon grated ginger
250ml/9fl oz full-fat milk
2 large free-range eggs
300g/9oz plain flour
1 tsp bicarbonate of soda,
   dissolved in 2 tbsp warm water

Makes: 10 slices
Prep time: 20 minutes
Cooking time: 45 minutes

1 Preheat oven to 170°C/325°F/GM3.

2 Melt the butter in a medium-sized saucepan and add the cinnamon and powdered ginger. Fry gently for a couple of minutes before adding the treacle, golden syrup, sugar and grated ginger.

3 While these are melting, mix together the milk and eggs, and put the flour in a separate large bowl.

4 In a small cup, mix together the bicarbonate of soda and warm water.

5 When the butter mixture has melted, mix in the milk and eggs.

6 Finally, pour all the wet ingredients (including the bicarbonate of soda) over the flour and mix well with a balloon whisk.

7 Divide the mixture between two non-stick 900g/2lb bread tins and bake for 45 minutes.

8 Place on a cooling rack and cool before slicing.

A naughty treat. My kids love the way the marshmallows go all gooey.

real hot chocolate with baby marshmallows

The real comfort of this is amazing - definitely worth rushing home from school for!

50g/2oz plain chocolate
300ml/11fl oz full-fat milk
mini-marshmallows (optional)

1 If you have a chance to think ahead, warm the jug a little first.

2 Break the chocolate up and put in the jug.

3 Bring the milk to the boil and pour about a quarter of it over the chocolate.

4 Leave the chocolate to melt for a minute, then whisk until smooth.

5 Return the remaining milk to the heat and bring back to the boil. As soon as it starts to boil, pour over the chocolate mixture, whisking all the time.

6 Serve immediately in small mugs or cups, sprinkling with as many marshmallows as you think necessary!

Makes: enough for two small mugs
Prep time: 1 minute
Cooking time: 4 minutes

apricot and oatbran muffins

These muffins are great to make in bulk and freeze individually. They will also stay fresh in an airtight container for a couple of days. The apricots keep them lovely and moist.

100g/4oz dried apricots
1 unwaxed lemon, zested and
    juiced
100g/4oz plain flour
75g/3½oz oatbran
1 tsp baking powder
250g/8oz butter/margarine
250g/8oz caster sugar
4 large free-range eggs, beaten
½ tsp cinnamon (optional)

1 Preheat oven to 180°C/350°F/GM4.

2 Start by blitzing the apricots in the food processor with the lemon juice and zest. If you don't have a food processor, simply cut the apricots as finely as you can and mix together with the lemon.

3 In another bowl, mix together the flour, oatbran and baking powder.

4 Ideally with an electric mixer or, if not, an electric hand-whisk, beat the butter and sugar together until white and fluffy. With the motor running, gradually add the beaten eggs.

5 Turn off the mixer and add half the flour, oatbran and baking powder mixture. Turn on the mixer to its lowest setting until the flour mixture is just mixed in. Scrape down the sides of the mixing bowl and add the remaining flour mixture and cinnamon. Mix gently until it is all incorporated.

6 Switch the mixer off again and add the mushed-up apricots and lemon.

7 Put the muffin cases into the tin, then spoon the mixture into the 12 muffin cases.

8 Bake for 20 minutes.

Makes: 12 muffins
Prep time: 20 minutes
Cooking time: 20 minutes

Tip

• A good breakfast treat if you are in a rush!

shortbread

There is something very comforting about a simple tin of plain shortbread. It's not flash or clever, but it can really work wonders after a long day at school. It also tastes fantastic with a mug of hot chocolate on a gloomy winter evening.

100g/4oz plain flour
50g/2oz cornflour
50g/2oz caster sugar
100g/4oz butter

Makes: 12 pieces
Prep time: 10 minutes
Cooking time: 25 minutes

1 Preheat oven to 160°C/310°F/GM2½. Grease and line a 20cm cake tin.

2 Sieve together the flour and cornflour in the bowl of the electric mixer. Add the sugar and then the butter. Turn the motor on to its lowest setting and watch as the mixture gradually becomes crumbly and then begins to come together in heavy lumps. At this point, turn the motor off and tip the mixture into the greased cake tin.

3 With the back of a dessert spoon, push the shortbread down into the cake tin. Flatten it as much as possible and then prick all over with a fork.

4 Bake for 25 minutes until the shortbread is cooked but not browned.

5 As soon as it comes out of the oven and while still in the tin, cut into 12 pieces and sprinkle lightly with caster sugar. Leave in the tin until cooled.

Tip

● Shortbread will keep fresh for a couple of days in an air-tight container. It will also freeze well, so it can be a good idea to make double quantities with this in mind.

almond and apricot yoghurt-coated bites

Sweet, chewy and oh-so-satisfying!

For the bites
75g/2½oz whole almonds
150g/5oz dried apricots
25g/1oz desiccated coconut
50g/2oz Rice Krispies
2tbsp golden syrup
50g/2oz soft dark sugar
50g/2oz margarine

For the icing
1 tbsp wholemilk yoghurt
50g/2oz cream cheese
200g/7oz icing sugar, sieved

1 Preheat oven to 170°C/325°F/GM3.

2 Start by roughly cutting the almonds in half lengthways. Roughly cut each apricot into about 6–8 pieces. In a large bowl, combine the almonds, apricots, coconut and Rice Krispies.

3 Put the golden syrup, sugar and margarine into a small saucepan. Melt together and then allow to boil vigorously for 1 minute.

4 Pour the syrup mixture over the dried ingredients and mix together, thoroughly coating everything with the sticky liquid.

5 Using a couple of dessert spoons, and before anything has a chance to set, quickly spoon the mixture onto the baking trays. Aim for each bite to be about 4cm in diameter.

6 Bake for 3 minutes. Leave to cool.

7 These taste delicious even without the yoghurt icing and will last for up to a week in an airtight container un-iced. For an even more delicious treat, though, slowly stir the yoghurt into the icing sugar. When it is fully combined, add the cream cheese. Initially the icing will go all lumpy, but just keep beating and it will soon sort itself out.

8 With a teaspoon, drizzle the icing over the cooled bites and allow to dry before eating.

Makes: approximately 30
Prep time: 20 minutes
Cooking time: 3 minutes

trying new tastes

The whole idea of this section is to encourage children to try new foods, and to help themselves to the right amount of food. Many children have eyes bigger than their stomachs – they see a pizza and want the whole thing. They don't naturally have the idea to take a little and then ask for seconds. The most common occurrence at parties or a family get-togethers is the amount of food left on plates by children – and also adults – who simply take too much!

The recipes in this section are intended to give you ideas for a table full of a selection of different foods, to encourage children to take a little of four or five items and try them – then maybe, if they are still hungry, to go back for more. The other important point I want to get across in this chapter is allowing children to use their fingers as well. We all constantly promote the use of cutlery, but there are times when it is OK to use fingers. For younger children this is a great time to get 'stuck in' with older siblings and feel part of the scene!

I tend to do this kind of lunch on a Saturday. I lay the table with a selection and make sure we have nice fresh bread, then let the children loose! The soups I include I serve in small cups, so the children can dip different things into them or simply have them as a starter – they love the idea of a meal with several different courses!

lettuce wraps and dippers

A bowl of crisp iceberg lettuce left in whole leaves makes a refreshing (and healthy) alternative to bread. The idea is that children can place a couple of items in as a filling, then roll the lettuce into a cigar shape and enjoy. This makes it slightly more fun and is not as filling as bread - it also encourages children to enjoy salad.

Baby gem lettuce is also a good idea as it is naturally sweet and, being so small, you can use them as spoons.

chunky guacamole

A great dish for children to make with you! Make sure the avocados are nice and ripe.

6 ripe avocados
2 limes, juice
small bunch of coriander, finely
    chopped
1 tbsp crème fraîche
½ tsp paprika
black pepper (optional)

Serves: 4 children + 2 adults
Prep time: 5 minutes

1 Slice the avocado open lengthways, remove the stone and skin and dice into a mixing bowl. Squeeze over the lime juice and toss in the coriander. Add the crème fraîche and paprika and mash with the back of a fork until a fairly smooth consistency. I also add a touch of black pepper to this.

Tip

• Personally, I like a chunky texture, but you can use a food processor for a smoother texture.

fool-proof houmous

350g/14oz chickpeas
   (tinned is fine)
3 tbsp tahini
1 garlic clove (crushed)
1 tbsp sesame oil
½ lemon, juice

Serves: 4 children + 2 adults
Prep time: 10 minutes

1 Place all the ingredients into a food processor and whiz until smooth. Add a little more lemon juice or a teaspoon of water if needed to make texture a little smoother.

crispy pancetta with mushrooms and spring onions

This is just a tasty salad to offer on your tableful of goodies. My children love pancetta but were always a little hesitant about mushrooms - mixing them with the pancetta has encouraged them to like mushrooms and taken away the classic snap decision 'I don't like it.' Sometimes it takes using things in different way to break a habit.

12 strips pancetta
8 button mushrooms, thinly sliced
4 spring onions, finely sliced

Serves: 4 children
Prep time: 15 minutes
Cooking time: 5 minutes
(for the pancetta)

1 Place the pancetta under the grill until nice and crispy, so you can literally just crush it into little pieces. Remove and place onto kitchen roll to absorb excess grease.

2 Crumble the pancetta into a small mixing bowl with the mushrooms and onions.

Tip

- I love serving this with a little creamy vinaigrette dressing, but it's just as tasty on its own.

- If you don't have any pancetta you can use streaky bacon.

bulgar and mint salad

This could not be easier and tastes wonderfully fresh. It also goes well with fish dishes.

200g/8oz bulgar wheat
   (cracked wheat)
salt
1 tsp allspice
250ml/9fl oz boiling water
4 spring onions, thinly sliced
½ cucumber, peeled and cubed
60g/2oz mint, chopped
40g/1½oz flat leaf parsley,
   chopped
1 lemon, juice
2 tbsp balsamic vinegar
4 tbsp extra virgin olive oil
salt and pepper

Serves: 4–6 children
(as part of a spread)
Prep/cooking time: 10 minutes
(but bulgar wheat needs 40 minutes
to absorb water)

1 Start by putting the bulgar in a small basin, sprinkling with a good pinch of salt and the allspice and pouring over the boiling water. Put a small plate or tin foil over the top of the bowl and allow the bulgar to absorb the water for about 40 minutes. Drain into a sieve.

2 Tip the bulgar into a larger bowl before adding the spring onions, cucumber, mint and parsley. Mix thoroughly.

3 Pour over the lemon juice, balsamic vinegar and olive oil and stir well. Check the seasoning before adding lots of freshly ground pepper and perhaps a little more salt.

cherry tomato and mozzarella salad

250g/10oz cherry tomatoes
1 tbsp extra-virgin olive oil
1 tbsp balsamic vinegar
2 tbsp fresh basil, finely chopped
10 baby mozzarella, sliced in half

Serves: 4–6 children/adults
(as part of a spread)
Prep time: 10 minutes

1 Slice the tomatoes into quarters and drizzle over the olive oil.

2 Add the balsamic vinegar and the basil. Gently stir all together and place into a small serving bowl.

3 The tomatoes are naturally very sweet, the vinegar and oil gently coat the tomatoes, complementing the taste and introducing children to the idea of dressing the tomatoes. The mozzarella is very mild in flavour and the perfect way to entice towards slightly grown-up salads.

classic prawn cocktail

This is a firm favourite.

200g/8oz cooked and peeled
    prawn
1 little gem lettuce, finely
    shedded
½ lime, juice
½ lemon, juice
1 tbsp mayonnaise
1 tbsp tomato ketchup
twist of black pepper

Serves: 4 children
Prep time: 15 minutes

1 Drain and empty the prawns into a mixing bowl along with the shredded lettuce. Pour in the lime and lemon juice and gently stir through the mayonnaise and ketchup, finishing with the twist of black pepper.

Tips

- Tasty additions include diced avocado or halved cherry tomatoes.

- I sometimes add some strips of smoked salmon to this – an additional treat!

soft-boiled eggs

- Boil for just 5 minutes and serve with the lettuce and a few other 'bits'. Once sliced open, the yolk mixes beautifully and acts as a salad dressing.

home deli temptations

Try not to assume your children won't like a particular taste or food, and always encourage them to try new things. We have a firm rule on our house - the children must not say, 'I don't like that,' until they have at least had a little taste. They amaze themselves at times. Jack, for example, adores marinated anchovies, which surprised me as they are quite a sophisticated taste for a little boy. He discovered them when he helped himself to one when I was making a salad for Gordon and me. I now put anchovies onto the table during these help-yourself lunches, along with other extras like grilled vegetables, sweet onions, dill pickles and pitted marinated olives.

some help-yourself favourites

- **Grilled Apricots** Lightly grill some dried apricots, this intensifies their flavour and softens them a little. They're lovely mixed into a salad.

- **Cheese Tasters** Vary your array of cheeses: some Double Gloucester, mature Cheddar, a nice mild creamy Brie, maybe even a mild blue cheese. Be careful to not just assume your children will not enjoy it – you will be surprised.

- **Cold Meat Medley** I love putting together cold meat platters from the deli. I mix several kinds of salami – napoli/milano/pepperoni – prosciutto, some honey roast ham, and let them help themselves! You can add anything to this; sometimes pork pie or corn beef are welcome additions. The whole idea is to vary it each time and introduce different tastes.

- **Fish** As well as anchovies, I like to put out some sardines and a seafood salad.

- **Grilled Vegetables** I like to use peppers, artichokes and aubergines. Simply drizzle a little olive oil over them and place under the grill, turning when they start to brown and soften.

smooth soups

You will need a liquidizer to make these delicious soups, but please be careful when you liquidize hot food – I have had several disasters where liquidizers have exploded! I suggest you leave the soup to cool slightly and always hold down the top of the liquidizer with a tea towel.

beetroot soup

This beautiful soup has a subtle, fragrant flavour. My children love it.

1kg/2.2lb raw beetroot
water
2 onions, sliced
1 celery stalk, sliced
1 carrot, sliced
1 tbsp olive oil
1½ litres/2½ pints chicken stock
   (or 1½ litres/2½ pints water
   with two quality chicken stock
   cubes)
1 tbsp plain flour
25g/1oz butter
½ lemon, juice
salt and pepper
150ml/5fl oz soured cream
30g/1oz bunch chives, chopped

Serves: 6
Prep time: 20 minutes
Cooking time: 1½ hours
approximately

1 Keeping the root and stem attached to the beetroot, place them in a large saucepan and cover with water. Bring to the boil and simmer for 40 minutes or until soft. Allow the beetroot to cool.

2 In another saucepan, fry the onions, celery and carrots in the olive oil for about 10 minutes, until beginning to soften.

3 Pour over the stock and bring to the boil. Simmer for 20 minutes.

4 The beetroot won't be completely cooked, so it will be slightly harder to slip their skins off. However, this is still possible if you cup your hands together around each beetroot and, using your thumbs, firmly push upwards around the beetroot, removing the skin as you go. It can be quite messy, so make sure you're wearing an apron.

5 Cut the beetroot into rough quarters and put in with the other vegetables and stock. Return the soup to the boil and simmer for 20 minutes.

6 Remove from the heat and allow to cool slightly before liquidizing in batches.

7 Return the puréed soup to the saucepan. Make a paste with the flour and butter and add to the soup. Stirring all the time, bring back to the boil and simmer for 5 minutes.

8 Pour in the lemon juice and season with salt and plenty of freshly ground black pepper.

9 Serve in warm bowls with a dessertspoon of soured cream and chopped chives.

pea and mint soup

This fresh, naturally sweet soup has a fantastic colour.

2 onions, sliced
1 tbsp olive oil
1 clove garlic, crushed
200g/8oz potatoes, diced
1½ litres/2½ pints chicken stock
500g/1lb frozen peas
30g/1oz mint
½ tsp caster sugar
250g/10oz pancetta, cubed, or
   bacon lardons

Serves: 6
Prep time: 25 minutes
Cooking time: 30 minutes

1 Fry the onions in the olive oil until soft without letting them colour. Add the garlic and potatoes. Cook for another couple of minutes.

2 Add the stock, bring to the boil and gently simmer for about 10 minutes until the potatoes are softening but not quite cooked.

3 Add the peas and approximately three-quarters of the mint. Bring back to the boil and simmer for about 3 minutes.

4 Remove from the heat and liquidize until smooth.

5 Return the soup to the heat, add the sugar and, about 5 minutes before you are ready to serve the soup, fry the cubed pancetta until beginning to crisp. I use a generous serving of pancetta, as we all love it, but do feel free to adjust the quantity to your taste.

6 Sprinkle the pancetta or lardons and remaining roughly torn mint onto the bowls of bright green soup and serve.

roasted butternut squash soup

This is a thick, velvety smooth soup that has the most incredibly bright and uplifting colour. It is fantastic served on a very cold, dull day.

2 x 2kg (4.4lb) butternut squash, quartered lengthways
1 tbsp groundnut oil
3 medium onions, sliced
50g/2oz butter
2 large garlic cloves, crushed
1½ litres/2½ pints chicken stock
500ml/18fl oz full-fat milk
nutmeg
salt and pepper
200g/8oz Gruyère or mature cheddar cheese, cubed
200ml/7fl oz crème fraîche
30g/1oz flat leaf parsley

1 Preheat oven to 180°C/350°F/GM4.

2 Take the quartered butternut squash and, using a dessert spoon, scrape out and discard all the seeds.

3 Put on a baking tray and brush all over with the groundnut oil. I find the easiest way of doing this is to pour a small dollop into the well of each quarter of squash and use my hands to make sure they are evenly coated.

4 Put in the oven and roast for 40 minutes.

5 In the meantime, in a large saucepan fry the onions in the butter and allow to turn golden. Add the garlic and fry for another couple of minutes before pouring on the stock. Bring to the boil and simmer for 20 minutes.

6 When the squash are ready, remove from the oven and allow to cool. Carefully scoop the flesh out of the skin and put in the hot stock. Bring to the boil again and simmer for a further 20 minutes.

7 Remove from the heat and liquidize well until it is a velvety smooth and bright orange.

8 Return to the saucepan; add the milk and a good grating of nutmeg. Season well with salt and pepper.

9 When ready to eat, divide the cubed cheese between warm bowls, pour over the soup and put a generous teaspoon of crème fraîche in each serving. Sprinkle with parsley and eat immediately.

Serves: 6
Prep time: 25 minutes
Cooking time: 2½ hours

curried parsnip and ginger soup

The sweetness of the parsnips and ginger make this a very popular soup for children. The curry flavour is not overwhelming, and is a very gentle way of introducing them to another dimension of flavours.

100g/4oz butter
2 medium onions, sliced
1kg/2.2lb parsnips, sliced
4cm piece of fresh ginger, grated
2 tsp garam masala
2 litres/3½ pints chicken stock
1 tbsp plain flour
2 cox apples, cored and cut into
   quarters
30g/1oz flat leaf parsley, coarsely
   chopped

Serves: 6
Prep time: 20 minutes
Cooking time: 40 minutes

Tip

• If you are making this soup for adults, substitute Bramley apples for the Coxes. I find the tartness of the Bramley apples cuts through the sweetness of the soup and makes it more appealing for an adult palate.

1 Melt a third of the butter in a large saucepan and add the onions. Fry on a medium heat for about 10 minutes until they are a golden colour. Stir regularly so they don't catch and burn.

2 Add the sliced parsnips and cook for another 5 minutes before adding the grated ginger and garam masala.

3 Continue to cook for another minute before adding the stock. Bring to the boil and simmer without a lid for 25 minutes.

4 Take the soup off the heat and allow to cool slightly before liquidizing in batches. You want the soup to be very smooth, so you might just want to check that there are no lumpy bits before pouring it back into the saucepan.

5 Take another third of the butter and the plain flour and mix to a paste in a cup with the back of a metal spoon.

6 Put the soup back on the heat and add the paste. Bring to the boil, stirring all the time. Reduce heat to a simmer.

7 While the soup is simmering, melt the remaining butter in the frying pan. Thinly slice the apple quarters, with the skin on, and fry in the butter.

8 As soon as the apples have begun to colour, serve the soup with the apple slices and chopped parsley scattered on top.

roasted sweet tomato and sweet pepper soup

The natural sweetness of roasted vine tomatoes is one of my favourite tastes in the whole world! By roasting the tomatoes and peppers you are intensifying their flavours. This is one of the things I always make if any of the children are off school ill. They snuggle up on the sofa with me and sip this soup and indulge in one-on-one attention for once.

3 tbsp olive oil
3 red peppers
3 yellow peppers
salt (Maldon is best) and pepper
200g/8oz vine cherry tomatoes
3 sprigs thyme
4 large onions, roughly chopped
2 cloves garlic, crushed
1 tsp cayenne pepper
2 tsp marjoram
2 tbsp fresh basil
1½ litres/2½ pints vegetable stock

Serves: 6
Prep time: 20 minutes
Cooking time: 1 hour

1 Preheat the oven to 180°C/350°F/GM4.

2 Lightly wipe two oven trays with a little olive oil.

3 Cut the peppers into quarters lengthways, remove core and seeds and lay onto oven tray. Add a little salt and black pepper and a drizzle of olive oil. Wash and place the tomatoes onto the other tray with the sprigs of thyme, a couple of twists of black pepper, sprinkle of Maldon salt, drizzle with a little oil and place in the oven.

4 These should roast for about 25 minutes, so they are soft and easy to pierce with the tip of a sharp knife.

5 While these are roasting, gently fry together the onions and garlic, add the cayenne pepper and marjoram – this becomes almost paste-like – and add these along with the tomatoes (removing the thyme stalk) and peppers into the food processor, with any juices, and the fresh basil. Whizz all together. Once processed you need to pass this mix through a mouli to get out any tomato seeds and skin.

6 Return the purée to the pan and add the stock, stirring all together. Leave to simmer for approximately 20–25 minutes. Serve.

cooking from
the cupboard

We all have days when we don't have the time or energy to go shopping. Before kids I used to just grab a bowl of cereal, but I can't get away with that now! I always try to keep a few staples in the house, such as eggs, dried pasta, bacon, frozen peas, long-life cream, potatoes, and tins of tomatoes, sardines, tuna and beans. I also like to keep fish and prawns in the freezer as they are easy to defrost and useful for any number of recipes. This means I can easily rustle up a meal whatever kind of day I've had.

These are my favourite emergency stock dishes. Don't worry if you don't have some of the ingredients as you can usually substitute them with something else (see the tips at the end of recipes). Cooking from the cupboard makes you more creative. You often end up matching different flavours you may not otherwise use – and with surprisingly good results!

homemade fish fingers with buttery mash and peas

This is a great recipe when you have no fresh food in the house and are desperate to come up with a comforting homemade meal!

2 eggs (for dipping the cod)
200g/7oz either shop-bought breadcrumbs or from the stale loaf lurking in the bottom of the bread bin!
552g/19oz cod (frozen)
6 medium potatoes
4 handfuls frozen peas
olive oil for greasing the baking tray
2 tbsp crème fraîche
knob of butter for the mash
2 tbsp whole milk
salt and pepper
2 tsp capers
1 gherkin, cut into ½cm cubes
4 tbsp mayonnaise

Serves: 4 children
Prep time: 30 minutes
Cooking time: 50 minutes

1 Preheat oven to 180°C/350°F/GM4.

2 Beat the eggs together and pour into a shallow dish.

3 If using a stale loaf, place the slices torn into chunks into a food processor (crusts left on, as this gives a lovely colour) and whizz until you have fine breadcrumbs.

4 Take the cod out of the freezer and cut into finger shapes. Place into the beaten egg and leave for a couple of minutes, turning to ensure all sides are coated.

5 Sprinkle the breadcrumbs onto a flat tray and take the fish fingers one at a time and roll them in the breadcrumbs.

6 Repeat until all are covered.

7 Place in the fridge for 20 minutes while you start the potatoes.

8 Peel the potatoes and place them in a saucepan of cold water (enough water just cover). Bring to the boil and simmer for approximately 20 minutes until softened. Ten minutes into the boiling time, place the frozen peas into the top steamer over the potatoes.

9   Meanwhile, place the fish fingers onto a lightly greased oven tray and place in the oven. Turn them over after approximately 15 minutes, carefully using a fish slice to ease any stuck sections.

10 Drain the potatoes and return them to the pan. Add the crème fraîche, butter, milk, salt and pepper and mash all through while warm.

11 Meanwhile, put the capers into a small mixing bowl and crush slightly with the back of a fork. Add the gherkin cubes and mayonnaise and stir through gently.

12 Check the fish fingers are cooked through, dish up the peas and mash, add a spoonful of the sauce on the side and serve.

Tips

- Sometimes I add a little twist to the mash by grating in some cheddar or parmesan cheese and stirring through.

- If you don't have any capers, simply mix 2 tbsp of mayonnaise with 2 tbsp of tomato ketchup to make a Marie Rose sauce.

spaghetti carbonara

Essential - all children love a nice bowl of pasta!

water for pasta
olive oil
300g/10oz spaghetti
2 egg yolks
75ml/2½fl oz double cream
75ml/2½fl oz half-fat crème
    fraîche
75g/3oz parmesan, finely grated
pepper
150g/5oz unsmoked streaky
    bacon or pancetta, sliced
1 tbsp olive oil
25g/1oz butter
small bunch flat leaf parsley,
    roughly chopped

Serves: 4 children
Prep time: 15 minutes
Cooking time: 25 minutes

1 Put the pasta water on to boil. When it comes to the boil, add the pasta and a bit of oil to keep the pasta from sticking. Stir frequently.

2 While the pasta is cooking, in a medium-sized bowl combine the egg yolks, double cream, crème fraîche, parmesan and a good grinding of pepper.

3 Fry the pancetta or bacon in the olive oil in a frying pan until it is just crispy. If using, pour over the dry Vermouth – being very careful because it will really bubble up. Remove from the heat until the pasta has cooked.

4 When the spaghetti is ready, drain it quickly and return it to the saucepan. Tip over the pancetta and the butter. Now, on the lowest possible heat, pour over the egg mixture and stir it through. Without taking your eye off it, keep stirring until it thickens to coat all the strands of spaghetti.

5 Serve with a little parsley sprinkled over each plate and some more parmesan for people to help themselves to.

Tip

- For a more adult twist, add 1 tbsp dry Vermouth, e.g. Noilly Prat, at stage 3.

- Remember to save the egg whites for meringues!

pea and parmesan risotto

A really simple risotto that always hits the spot.

1.2 litres/2 pints chicken or
    vegetable stock
100g/4oz unsalted butter
2 medium onions, finely chopped
1 clove garlic, crushed
225g/7½oz Arborio (risotto) rice
100g/4oz frozen peas
50g/2oz parmesan cheese, finely
    grated

1 Start by putting the stock in a saucepan and bringing to the boil. Keep it on a very low heat while you are making the risotto.

2 In the sauté pan, melt the butter and add the onions and garlic. Allow to cook for 5 minutes.

3 Add the rice and stir continuously over a low heat until the grains start to soften.

4 Over a medium heat begin to add the hot stock, a ladle at a time. It is important to allow the rice to absorb all the stock before adding any more.

5 Continue to add the stock gradually, stirring all the time while the pan bubbles happily for about 15–20 minutes. The rice is ready when it is soft but still has a slight chalky 'bite' to it in the middle.

6 You can, if you feel inclined, cook the frozen peas before adding to the risotto, but personally I prefer to save on the washing up! I therefore simply tip the frozen peas straight into the risotto and stir in. After about 3 minutes the peas should be defrosted and the risotto bubbling again.

7 Finally, stir in the grated parmesan and serve immediately in warm bowls with some very thinly sliced parmesan sprinkled on top, a big bowl of rocket salad and warm crusty bread.

Serves: 4–6
Prep time: 10 minutes
Cooking time: 25–30 minutes

Tip

- When I say 1.2 litres of chicken or vegetable stock, all I really mean is 1.2 litres of water and two good-quality stock cubes. I do try and make my own chicken stock and freeze it, but it is still easier in certain situations to use a stock cube!

corned beef hash

I have to say I am not the biggest fan of this dish, but Jack adores it, as does Gordon. A classic example of having to put aside my personal taste and not discourage Jack and the girls just because I don't like something!

125g/4½oz potatoes
   (I use organic red potatoes)
125g/4½oz carrots
drizzle of olive oil
1 medium onion, sliced
1 clove garlic, crushed
250g/8oz corned beef
pinch of cayenne pepper
small pinch of salt
1 tbsp stock (if desired)
1 tbsp parsley, chopped

Serves: 4 children
Prep time: 10 minutes
Cooking time: 25 minutes

1 Boil the potatoes and steam the carrots over the top of the saucepan.

2 Meanwhile, heat the olive oil in a large frying pan and fry the sliced onion and crushed garlic until softened (about 10 minutes). Add the corned beef.

3 When the potatoes and carrots are finished, rinse off so they are cool enough to handle. Chop them into cubes of approximately 1–2cm and add to the corned beef mixture. Stir all gently together and add the cayenne pepper and a small pinch of salt.

4 Let the mix get a little browned, but keep turning so everything becomes a little crispy. Make sure it is hot throughout. I sometimes add a small touch of stock as I prefer it a little moist, but I know the traditional way is to eat the hash a little crispy!

5 Sprinkle through the parsley just before serving.

Tips

- I love to serve this with crusty bread and butter.

- Delicious with a little tomato ketchup on the side!

- Garden peas suit this dish.

butter bean and chorizo stew

A fantastically hearty meal made mostly from cupboard items, so great for a last-minute supper if you come home to an empty fridge.

15 strands saffron or ½ tsp
   turmeric
1 tbsp boiling water
310g/11oz chorizo (skinned)
olive oil
400g/14oz tin of whole red
   pimientos
1 medium onion
1 clove garlic
½ tsp paprika
½ tsp ground cumin
100g/4oz sundried tomatoes,
   chopped
100g/4oz Borette onions (baby sweet
   onions marinated in balsamic
   vinegar), chopped into quarters
200g/7oz tin chopped tomatoes
   in sauce
400g/14oz tin butter beans
75g/3oz pitted black olives
sprig of rosemary

Serves: 4 hungry children
Prep time: 20 minutes
Cooking time: 45 minutes

1 Soak the saffron in a small bowl with a tablespoon of boiling water.

2 Cut up the chorizo into chunks, fry over a high heat with a drizzle of olive oil, letting it sweat out its lovely orange colour. This takes about 5 minutes. Remove and put aside. Lightly fry the pimientos until slightly browned, remove and place aside with the chorizo.

3 Fry the onion and garlic until softened, add the paprika and cumin and continue to gently fry for a couple of minutes. Add the sundried tomatoes and marinated onions, frying together. Add the chopped tomatoes, saffron and the water it was soaking in plus another 300ml water and bring all to the boil.

4 Turn the heat down to a simmer, add the butter beans, stir all together and bring back to the boil. Turn down to a simmer, add the chorizo and cook for approximately 30 minutes.

5 Just before serving, add and stir in the pimientos and pitted black olives, and finally, sprinkle over the rosemary.

Tip

- Lovely served over either basmati rice or with a jacket potato.

- Also delicious with a spoonful of crème fraîche stirred in just before serving.

- If you don't have any chorizo, any spicy sausage will do. Ordinary pickled onions will also work.

macaroni cheese with tomato and crispy bacon

A delicious macaroni cheese with a twist of tomato and crispy bacon.

25g/1oz butter
25g/1oz plain flour
½ tsp cayenne pepper
285ml/½ pint whole milk
300g/10oz macaroni
400g/14oz tin chopped tomatoes,
    drained
250g/8oz grated medium cheddar
200g/7oz unsmoked streaky
    bacon, cut into strips

Serves: 4 children
Prep time: 15 minutes
Cooking time: 40 minutes

1 Preheat grill to hot.

2 Put a pan of water on to boil.

3 Start making a basic white sauce: Melt the butter in a medium saucepan and add the flour. Stir it around and let it form a paste. As the paste starts look as if it's drying (but has not yet browned), add the cayenne pepper and stir for another minute. Gradually add the milk while beating with a small whisk all the time. Bring to the boil, stirring all the time, and allow to simmer for a couple of minutes. The sauce should easily coat the back of a wooden spoon.

4 When the pasta water has come to the boil, add the macaroni and cook for about 2 minutes less than the instructions on the packet. Drain in a sieve and put to one side until needed.

5 When your white sauce has simmered for a couple of minutes, add the drained tomatoes. Remove the sauce from the heat and put to one side for about a minute before adding 150g/5oz of the grated cheddar. Finally add the drained macaroni and mix together.

6 Pour the macaroni mixture into the ovenproof dish and cover with the pieces of bacon. Finally sprinkle over the remaining cheese.

7 Place under the grill for about 10 minutes until the bacon has turned crispy and slightly burnt at the edges.

8 Serve with a crisp green salad.

tinned sardines with avocado on toast

My children love sardines - I think this is partly because it fascinates them that they can eat the little bones!

If ever the children are not well, they quite often request this for lunch. The avocado is lovely and soft and comforting - it's also a natural moisturizer and can help with dry skin.

2 x 120g/4½oz tins of sardines
2 avocados (nice and ripe)
4 slices wholemeal bread
4 tsp mayonnaise
2 plum tomatoes, sliced (optional)
2 spring onions, finely chopped
   (optional)
1 lemon, cut into quarters
twist of black pepper

Serves: 4
Prep time: 15 minutes
Cooking time: 5–6 minutes

1 Drain the sardines into a sieve over the sink. Cut the avocados in half lengthways, remove the stone and take off the skin. Slice the avocados again, lengthways.

2 Toast the bread then spread each slice with a teaspoon of mayonnaise on one side, then lay half a sliced avocado onto this, then 4 sardines.

3 Slice the plum tomatoes, lay a couple of slices on top of the sardines, sprinkle with the finely chopped spring onions and place under the grill for approximately 5–6 minutes – it is hard to time this one, as with anything you grill, just keep an eye on it.

4 When it is ready, drizzle with lemon, a twist of black pepper and you are ready!

prawns with chilli and cheese

I love introducing my children to slightly spicy foods, and this is a great dish for that as the spice is softened by the cheese. It sounds a strange combination, but it tastes delicious!

300g/10oz frozen raw prawns,
    without heads or shells,
    defrosted. Tiger prawns are
    delicious.
1 lime, juice
tabasco
2 tbsp olive oil
1 medium red onion, thinly sliced
2 cloves garlic, crushed
2 fresh red chillies/½ tsp chilli
    flakes
salt and pepper
200ml/7fl oz double cream (long-
    life is quite acceptable)
125g/3½oz mozzarella cheese
1 bag fresh coriander, roughly
    chopped

Serves: 2
Prep time: 15 minutes
Cooking time: 20 minutes

1 Preheat grill to hot.

2 Make sure the prawns are completely defrosted. I think they defrost fastest in a sieve, occasionally turning a cold tap on them to hurry things up a bit. Once they are ready, put in a bowl and cover with the lime juice and a couple of splashes of tabasco. Leave for 10–15 minutes.

3 Heat the olive oil in a pan and add the red onion and garlic. Gently cook for about 3 minutes before adding the chillis. Continue to cook for a further 2 minutes.

4 Divide the onion mixture between the two gratin dishes. Drain the prawns and divide these equally, too.

5 Season well before pouring over the cream, followed by the mozzarella sprinkled on top.

6 Place under the grill for about 10 minutes until the cheese is bubbling and brown and the prawns are pink.

7 Serve with the coriander scattered on top, and a loaf of fresh French bread.

pasta with tomato and egg sauce

This has become a regular favourite - the children love all pasta, but this is a real comfort meal!

1 medium onion, finely chopped
1 tbsp olive oil
1 clove garlic, crushed
400g/14oz tin chopped tomatoes
1 tsp dried oregano
1 large organic egg
8 nests tagliatelle
salt and pepper
1 tsp caster sugar (optional)

Serves: 4 children
Prep time: 5 minutes
Cooking time: 30 minutes

1 Start by frying the chopped onion in the oil in a medium saucepan for about 5 minutes before adding the garlic. Add the tin of tomatoes and bring to the boil. Add the oregano. Simmer on a low heat with the lid on for about 30 minutes.

2 While this is happening, beat the egg and put the pasta water on to boil. When boiling, throw in the tagliatelle, bring back to the boil then let simmer.

3 Just before the tagliatelle is ready (after about 5 minutes), stir the beaten egg into the tomato sauce, stirring all the time so that the egg doesn't go all lumpy. The idea is to have a relatively smooth and creamy sauce. Once the egg has cooked through (this shouldn't take more than a minute or two), take the sauce off the heat. Check the seasoning, and, if you think necessary, add a teaspoon of sugar.

4 Drain the pasta and stir in the sauce.

5 Serve with grated cheese.

rice pudding

I was put off rice pudding by the terrible version I was always served at school. However, by making it for my own children I have learned to enjoy it once again!

25g/1oz butter
110g/4½oz pudding rice
400g/14oz tin light evaporated
   milk
500ml/18fl oz whole milk
40g/1½oz golden granulated sugar
½ nutmeg
quality all-fruit jam

Serves: 4–6
Prep time: 5 minutes
Cooking time: 2 hours

1 Preheat oven to 150°C/300°F/GM2.

2 Generously grease an ovenproof dish with the butter.

3 Put the rice, evaporated milk, whole milk and sugar into the dish and stir well.

4 Finely grate the nutmeg over the pudding.

5 Pop into the middle of the oven and, after 30 minutes, give it all a good stir. Bake for another 30 minutes and stir through again. Leave to bake for another hour.

6 Divide into bowls with a big blob of jam in the middle.

peaches with cinnamon, cardamom and vanilla ice cream

This is a very quick, 'not much time to think about it' dessert that was created by a friend of mine when we used to cook each other dinner after a hectic day at work (we never had much in the cupboard'). We now both have children and make it for them when stuck for fresh ingredients.

1 400g/14oz tin of peaches
1 cinnamon stick
4 cardamom pods
4 scoops vanilla ice cream
   (my favourite is Mackies
   organic)

Serves: 4 children
Prep time: 5 minutes
Cooking time: 25 minutes

1 Preheat the oven to 160°C/325°F/GM3.

2 Pour the peaches and their syrup/juice into a shallow ovenproof dish. Add the cinnamon stick and slightly crush the cardamom pods and add them, too. Put the dish into the oven leave slowly cooking for approximately 25 minutes.

3 Serve with a scoop of ice cream, taking care to remove the cardamom pods from the portions first. Deliciously easy!

Tip

- If you don't have any cardamom in the cupboard add ¼ tsp of nutmeg or Allspice instead.

after-school
suppers

Meal times have become really important in our house. Somehow, once my children learned to feed themselves I started to chat to them distractedly, whizzing around the kitchen doing other jobs and, more often than not, only half-listening. This really did me no favours, as the children would get frustrated and irritable. It made me realize that it was totally unfair of me to expect them to have good table manners and to talk about their day when I was not bothering to give them my full attention. I now make sure that when I am at home, I sit and just have a cup of tea with them while they eat supper, and really listen to them talking about their day.

This makes a real difference both to manners and attitude at the table, and means that by the end of supper the children have relaxed and are content. I find that mealtimes seem to be the moment when my children are more sociable and willing to discuss their day. Although at bedtime I will sit with each one of them individually, they usually seem too tired for any real discussion and simply want the comfort of a story and a cuddle!

Of course it's not always possible to get home for tea time, but I think it is crucial to ensure that you have 'catch up' time as a family at some point during the week, or at the weekends at dinner or lunch, and encourage the children to ask and listen to your news as well as telling you about theirs.

As this can easily be one of the trickiest times of the day – the children are likely to be hungry, grumpy and over-tired – I find it's best to have a quick or at least partially prepared meal. I know that with working hours and the demands of other children this is not always possible, but if your children are anything like mine they're having their lunch at school, so I feel it's extra-important that they get a very healthy and nutritious supper. I have chosen dishes here that are all fairly quick and easy to put together. Some have longer cooking times, but this allows you to help with homework or give the children your undivided attention while things are cooking away!

Tip

- Try to plan your week of suppers in advance – this saves having to keep going to the shops for bits and pieces. You will also find it easier to keep to a budget if you plan in advance, as you won't have so many leftovers or be tempted to buy items on a whim!

- Where possible, partially prepare bits of supper the night before. My evenings often feel as if they are spent preparing for the next day, but when the children are in bed you get things done a lot quicker, and this makes the next day much easier.

chicken and butter bean casserole with basmati rice

This dish was made up when supper was running really late one night and one of the children groaned when I suggested having chicken. When quizzed on why that was a problem, the answer came winging back that they always found chicken too hard to eat as it needed more sauce. The perfect recipe was created – quick, easy and no complaints since!

drizzle of olive oil
4 small red onions, finely
    chopped
1 clove of garlic, crushed
2 sticks celery, finely sliced
1 sweet red pepper, finely sliced
    and seeded
6 baby leeks, finely sliced
6 portabellini mushrooms
    (or any large flat mushrooms)
1½ litres/3 pints chicken stock
2 tbsp soy sauce
1 tin (400g/14oz) chopped
    tomatoes
2 carrots, finely diced
1 tin (400g/14oz) butter beans
10 chicken thighs on the bone,
    skin removed
water
285g/10oz basmati rice

1 Heat the olive oil in a large heavy-bottomed saucepan. Add the onions and garlic and fry gently until softened. Add the celery, red pepper, leeks and mushrooms, gently stirring together. Add the stock, soy sauce and tomatoes and bring to the boil. Turn down to a gentle simmer.

2 Add the carrots and butter beans. Add the chicken thighs whole and leave all to simmer gently for approximately 1 hour.

3 Bring to the boil a pan of water seasoned with a pinch of salt. Add the basmati rice – always hard to find the right amount, but I usually judge it at ½ mug of dried rice per child. Prepare as per the directions on the packet.

4 Take out one of the chicken thighs and gently break it open. Check the meat is all cooked.

5 Drain the rice and serve into bowls.

6 Remove a chicken thigh, one per portion, and remove the bone. The chicken should literally fall off the bone. If desired, cut into bite-sized pieces.

7 Add a generous ladle of vegetables and sauce, and serve.

Serves: 6 children + leftovers!
Prep time: approximately 25 minutes
Cooking time: approximately 1 hour

Tips

- A great way to maintain all the goodness from the veg and meat, as it is all slow-cooked within the stock. The rice absorbs some sauce as well.

- You can prepare the base of stock and veg in advance and reheat, adding the meat later on and simmering as directed.

- This is a great recipe for fish as well: simply replace the chicken with a chunky fish like cod or monkfish. You would simmer the veg for approximately half an hour until tender, then add the fish and simmer for another 10 minutes until cooked through.

- To turn this dish around for adult suppers, simply add a little Worcester sauce and black pepper and mix through.

fish chowder

A lovely creamy soup, incredibly filling. It's easy to slip in extra vegetables, and this is a really nice alternative to traditional fish pie.

knob of butter
3 tbsp olive oil
250g/½lb bacon, cut into small
  strips
4 medium potatoes
3 large leeks, thinly sliced
3 large onions, finely sliced
1½ litres/2½ pints good chicken
  stock
500g/1lb smoked haddock
500g/1lb chunky cod
handful frozen peas
handful frozen sweetcorn
450ml/¾ pint double cream
1 tsp flat parsley to top when
  serving (optional)

Serves: 8 children + seconds!
Prep time: 20 minutes
Cooking time: 30 minutes

1 Heat the butter and olive oil with the bacon in a large pan and fry until a little crispy. Meanwhile, peel and chop the potatoes into bite-sized pieces and boil in enough water to cover until just a little underdone. Drain and put aside.

2 Add the leeks and onions to the bacon and cook until soft.

3 Add the chicken stock and potatoes to the pan and bring to the boil.

4 Lower the heat and simmer for approximately 10 minutes.

5 Add the fish, peas and sweetcorn and let simmer until the fish is cooked. This takes approximately 10–15 minutes.

6 Lastly, add the double cream and stir through until the soup is simmering again. Finely chop the flat parsley and sprinkle into the pan, stirring through.

7 Dish up into bowls and serve.

Tips

- If you were serving this for adults you would add 12 scallops and a couple of pinches of Maldon sea salt.

- For a dinner party, add a tablespoon of plain flour to the vegetables once they have softened – this absorbs some of the oil and stops oil bubbles floating on the top. Purely for visual reasons!

- This soup can be made in advance and frozen by just making the base ingredients (stock and vegetables) and freezing; then you only need to defrost, reheat and add the fish and cream.

lime and ginger salmon fillets with noodles

Salmon is very popular with my children. It has quite a delicate flavour and is not as strong as some other kinds of fish in smell or taste. The marinade is deliciously sticky and really complements the salmon.

2 tbsp runny honey
1 tbsp grain mustard
2cm grated fresh ginger
2 limes, juice
1 lime, zest
500g/1lb fresh salmon fillets
    (skinless and boneless)
broccoli florets
    (approx 3 per child)
250g/8oz fine egg noodles
2 knobs of butter

Serves: 4 children
Prep time: 15 minutes
Cooking time: 15 minutes

1 Mix together the honey, mustard, ginger and lime juice and zest. Cut the salmon fillets into four portions and leave to marinate in the honey/lime mixture for at least 15 minutes.

2 Meanwhile, bring to the boil a pan of water to steam the broccoli and cook the noodles. Cook the noodles as directed on the packet. The broccoli takes approximately 10 minutes, until you can easily pierce the stalk with a sharp knife and the floret goes a lovely bright green.

3 Heat the first knob of butter in a frying pan until slightly bubbling. Remove the salmon from the marinade with a slotted spoon (retaining the marinade) and place in the frying pan. The heat should be fairly high and the fillets should take approximately 3–4 minutes each side to cook through. Once cooked, place to one side.

4 Add the other knob of butter to the pan on a high heat. Let it melt and bubble, then pour in the remaining marinade. Bring to the boil and let it reduce for approximately 1 minute.

5 Place the salmon on the noodles and tip over the marinade. Serve the broccoli alongside.

Tips

- I find limes easier to juice if you roll them on a chopping board before slicing open.

- This dish is great with rice, too.

chicken breast with red lentil sauce

A comforting dish that goes down particularly well in the winter, especially after swimming lessons when the children are cold and tired but need a hearty tea.

1 medium onion, finely chopped
4 tbsp olive oil
1 clove garlic
200g/7oz carrots, sliced
75g/3oz red lentils
1 tbsp tomato purée
1 tsp harissa paste (optional)
400g/14oz tin chopped tomatoes
300ml/11fl oz water
250g/8oz Basmati rice
3 chicken breasts
1 tsp soft brown sugar
salt and pepper
handful flat leaf parsley, chopped

Serves: 4 children
Prep time: 15 minutes
Cooking time: 50 minutes

1 To make the sauce, gently fry the onion in half of the oil until soft. Add the sliced garlic and continue to fry for further 2 minutes.

2 Add the carrots and fry on a low heat for another 5 minutes before stirring in the red lentils. Add the tomato purée and harissa paste and coat all the vegetables before adding the tomatoes and water. Simmer this all on a low heat with the lid on for 40 minutes.

3 When the sauce is cooked, pass through a medium-graded mouli or push through a sieve, using the back of a wooden spoon to help.

4 The sauce is now ready and can be frozen or refrigerated until needed.

5 When you are ready to cook, start by putting the rice on to simmer in a pan of boiling water.

6 Chop up the chicken breasts into 2cm cubes. In a heavy-bottomed saucepan, fry the chicken in the remaining olive oil until it has coloured and is going slightly golden at the edges.

7 Pour the sauce over the chicken and bring to the boil. Put the lid on the saucepan and simmer for 10 minutes.

8 Serve with the rice and flat leaf parsley.

Tip

* I always make this sauce in advance, usually doubling the quantities and freezing half for future use.

baked pumpkin and fresh pea risotto

This is one of my favourites, simply because it is so easy to make - you quite simply put it all into an oven-proof dish and pop into the oven, allowing you to get on with other things (like helping with homework!).

400g/14oz risotto rice
1¼ litres/2 pints chicken stock
50g/2oz butter
500g/1lb pumpkin, peeled and
    chopped into cubes
12 slices pancetta, or unsmoked
    streaky bacon
handful of fresh peas
250g/½lb grated parmesan
1 tbsp flat parsley

Serves: 6 children
Prep time: 10 minutes
Cooking time: 30 minutes

1 Place the rice, stock, butter and pumpkin in an oven-proof dish, cover tightly with either a lid or foil and bake in for 30 minutes at 200°C/400°F/GM6.

2 Meanwhile, place the pancetta under the grill until crispy. Lay it onto some kitchen roll to absorb any excess oil.

3 Take out the risotto and remove the lid. Stir through, making sure to relieve any bits stuck on the bottom. There will still be some liquid, but this will be absorbed. Sprinkle in the fresh peas and stir through. They will cook in the stock very quickly (approx 3–4 minutes). Sprinkle over the parmesan, stir all through. This will now thicken.

4 Dish into bowls and lay the pancetta over the top, either whole or broken into pieces.

5 Sprinkle over the flat parsley and serve.

Tips

- Cheddar cheese could be used, but will taste a little heavier. Maybe half cheddar and half parmesan if preferred.

- Fresh peas add fantastic natural sweetness and colour to this dish, but broad beans or sweetcorn would also work.

pasta sauces

Pasta is a quick and easy option - especially if I'm running late. These are my two favourite sauces.

amatriciana

2 tbsp olive oil
200g/8oz unsmoked streaky
   bacon, diced
2 medium onions, finely diced
½ tsp chilli flakes
400g/14oz tin chopped tomatoes
½ tsp dried oregano
50ml/2fl oz red wine
175g/7oz dried penne or rigatoni
25g/1oz butter
pepper
1 tbsp grated parmesan

Serves: 6 with pasta
Prep time: 15 minutes
Cooking time: 25 minutes

1 Bring a large pan of salted water to the boil.

2 Heat the oil in a large frying pan on a moderate heat and add the bacon. Fry for about 5 minutes, allowing the fat to run before adding the onions and chilli flakes. Cook for a further 15 minutes, stirring all the time to prevent anything catching.

3 Add the tinned tomatoes, wine and oregano and bring to the boil.

4 As you turn the sauce down to a very gentle simmer, put the pasta into the boiling water. Cook the pasta until just tender, drain and return to the saucepan. Pour over the sauce and stir in the butter.

5 Serve at once sprinkled with lots of pepper and parmesan.

pesto

I prefer to make fresh pesto in high summer when it is possible to buy great bunches of strong, verdant basil fresh from Italy. Somehow supermarket basil never does the job as well. The flavour of the pesto is completely dependant on the quality of the basil, so I think this should be a seasonal sauce.

2 tbsp pine nuts
100g/4oz fresh basil leaves
2 large cloves garlic, crushed
12 tbsp extra virgin olive oil
salt
75g/3oz parmesan, grated

Serves: 6 with pasta
Prep time: 15 minutes
Cooking time: 20 minutes

1 Bring a large pan of salted water to the boil.

2 Start by dry-frying the pine nuts in a non-stick frying pan. You need to watch them all the time because once they start changing colour they burn very quickly. As soon as they have turned a golden brown, tip out into a bowl and allow to cool.

3 Put the pasta into the boiling water and leave to cook until just tender. Drain and return to the saucepan.

4 Meanwhile put the basil, garlic, cooled pine nuts, olive oil and pinch of salt in the goblet of a food processor. Blitz until you have a smooth paste.

5 Pour the mixture into a bowl and stir in the grated parmesan.

6 Pour over the drained pasta and serve immediately with lots of black pepper.

Tip

- If you want to store this in the fridge for 24 hours, pour into a jam jar, shake the jar to flatten the surface of the pesto and pour over enough olive oil to make sure it is well covered.

sausage casserole with savoy cabbage and butter beans

I love this dish and the more I make it, the more I think of different things to put in! It's a good hearty casserole, and one of the few ways I can get my children to enjoy cabbage (and on occasions I slip in sprouts, too!).

2 tbsp olive oil
2 medium onions, finely chopped
1 clove garlic (crushed)
500g/1lb sausages
55g/3oz cubed pancetta, or bacon lardons
4 baby leeks, finely sliced
2 sprigs fresh thyme
55g/3oz chorizo sausage, cut into chunky bite-sized pieces
235g/7½oz butter beans (drained)
1½ litres/2½ pints vegetable stock
8 mushrooms (medium flat mushrooms), sliced
1 Savoy cabbage, shredded and core removed

Serves: 6 children with leftovers
Prep time: 30 minutes
Cooking time: 40 minutes
(though the longer the better)

1 Gently heat the olive oil in a deep pan. Add the onions and garlic and fry until softened. Add the sausages and gently brown. Add the pancetta, leeks and thyme. Put in the chorizo and turn the heat up slightly so that it sweats off some of the oil. This gives the leeks and onions a lovely orange colour.

2 Add the butter beans, stock, and mushrooms. Bring this all to the boil, turn down and simmer for approximately 15 minutes.

3 Cut the Savoy cabbage in half through the centre root, remove the root area and cut into shreds. Add all of this to the pan – it may look too much but it does soften and mix in. Stir it all through and leave to all simmer for as long as possible, at least 25 minutes. The longer the better.

4 Serve.

Tips

- This is lovely served with rice, but substantial enough without, too.

- I sometimes use up the end of a French baguette that has been left from the day before with this dish, by slicing it in half, topping it with grated cheddar cheese and grilling it.

king prawn and monkfish curry

The coconut milk sweetens this dish and softens the chilli, while the cashew nuts add a lovely texture, but are purely optional.

drizzle vegetable oil
1 large onion, finely chopped
1 clove garlic, crushed
1cm fresh ginger, grated
1 small red chilli, finely chopped
   and deseeded
1 tsp tumeric
1 tsp ground cumin
1tsp ground coriander
2 cardamom pods, bruised
400ml/16fl oz tin coconut milk
500ml/½ pint chicken stock
100g/4oz French beans
700g/1lb 7oz basmati rice
drizzle olive oil
500g/1lb tiger prawns
750g/1½lb monkfish tail, cut into
   bite-sized pieces
handful cashew nuts, toasted
small bunch of fresh coriander
4 tbsp soured cream

Serves: 6 children
Prep time: 20 minutes
Cooking time: 40 minutes

1 Add vegetable oil to a large saucepan and gently fry the onion and garlic until softened. Add all the spices and stir together – this becomes a sticky paste! Add the coconut milk and the stock and bring to the boil – then simmer for approximately 20 minutes.

2 Add the French beans, cut in half. Cook for a further 10 minutes until the beans are slightly softened.

3 Place the rice into a pan of boiling water, cook as directed on the packet, drain and stir through a little olive oil.

4 Meanwhile, lightly toast the cashew nuts in a frying pan.

5 Add the prawns and monkfish to the large saucepan with the curry mixture, and the toasted cashew nuts. Bring back to the boil and simmer for 5 minutes until the prawns and monkfish are cooked.

6 Finely chop the coriander, add to the pan and stir in the sour cream. Leave to simmer for a further 3 minutes.

7 Serve the rice into bowls and top with curry.

Tips

- This is great as a chicken curry, too. Just adjust the cooking time for longer.

- Using the tail end of monkfish makes this dish a little cheaper, and also a little meatier.

This recipe's a great way to introduce children to spicy food.

plaice with chunky chips and pea purée

Fish and chips, a classic dish. I do this with pea purée, as Jack had a real thing about peas - quite odd as they really are so small, sweet tasting and harmless. However, he adores pea purée, and was very proud that he had enjoyed it so much when he watched me making it and realized it was literally just peas mashed up. Also, the purée acts almost like a sauce, or 'green ketchup' as they love to call it.

4 medium-sized potatoes,
   scrubbed, skin left on
handful plain flour for coating
   the fillets
4 fillets of plaice

For the pea purée
70g/2½oz butter
1 small onion, peeled and
   finely chopped
1kg/2.2lb frozen peas
200ml/7fl oz vegetable stock
10g/½oz mint leaves
pinch of salt and pepper

1 Preheat oven to 190°C/375°F/GM5.

2 Cut the potatoes into chunky chips, then boil for approximately 20 minutes – until they have very slightly softened.

3 Drain and put onto a lightly oiled roasting tray. Place into the oven for approximately 25 minutes, until golden and crispy.

4 Meanwhile, for the pea purée, heat a third of the butter in a small pan and add the onion, cooking it until it softens. Add the peas, vegetable stock and mint leaves. Add the seasoning and simmer for 10 minutes.

5 Blend this in a food processor, return to the pan and stir through the rest of the butter.

6 For the plaice, put the flour onto a large flat plate and lay both sides of the fillets into this until lightly covered.

7 Heat a knob of butter in a large frying pan and fry each fillet skin-side down first for approximately 4 minutes each side, getting the skin as crisp as possible.

8 Serve on a plate with a couple of chips each and a spoonful of pea purée.

Serves: 4 children
Prep time: 15 minutes
Cooking time: 35 minutes

Tip

- Sometimes I also make a little dipping sauce of mayonnaise and slightly crushed capers and diced gherkin – a sort of tartare sauce. Simply squash the capers and stir through a little mayonnaise – an acquired taste for a child, but, like grain mustard and olives, some children simply adore it! I use this with my homemade fishfinger recipe in Cooking from the Cupboard.

- If you are cooking more fish than will fit in the frying pan, cook each piece for 2–3 minutes then put on a baking sheet and finish in a hot oven for a few minutes with a knob of butter.

- Boiling the chips first makes them fluffy on the inside and crispy on the outside. It also cooks them quicker.

tagliatelle with veal, orange and thyme

I love to mix sweet flavours such as orange juice into savoury dishes. It always surprises me that we naturally seem to keep the flavours apart. It is a recipe that I often have to hand over because the friend goes home talking about it – I take it as a huge compliment when a child loves my cooking, as when they don't they are never too shy to let you know!

2 large veal escalopes
4 nests of tagliatelle
1 tbsp olive oil
150ml/5fl oz freshly squeezed
   orange juice
1 tbsp crème fraîche
1 tbsp fresh thyme, chopped
25g/1oz butter
1 bunch flat leaf parsley, chopped
salt and pepper to season

1 The veal escalopes need to be about 3mm thick. Usually my butcher does this for me, but if not, put the meat between two pieces of greaseproof paper and hit with a rolling pin until they are the right thickness.

2 Have your oven preheated to 110°C/225°F/ GM¼ so that you can keep the veal warm while sorting out the pasta. Just before you start cooking the meat, put the tagliatelle nests into a pan of boiling water.

3 Heat the olive oil in a large frying pan on a high heat. When the oil starts to shimmer, place the veal very carefully into the pan. Cook for about 2 minutes before turning the escalopes over and cooking the other side. Cook for a further 2 minutes. As soon as the meat is cooked, put on a plate in a warm oven. Add the orange juice to the pan, stirring to remove any residue from the pan bottom. When the juice has reduced a little, stir in the crème fraîche, thyme and butter. Mix it all together and simmer for a minute or two while you drain the tagliatelle and stir in the parsley. Season to taste.

4 Serve the pasta onto plates. Return the veal to the sauce and serve over the tagliatelle.

Serves: 4 children
Prep time: 10 minutes
Cooking time: 15 minutes

cauliflower and broccoli cheese

Real nursery food with a slight twist - bacon! My children often feel a little short-changed if they don't have just a little meat in a meal. If we have any vegetarian friends for tea, we can all eat the same with additions as desired, without making it twice the work.

water
8 rashers unsmoked streaky
    bacon or pancetta slices
50g/2oz butter
50g/2oz plain flour
400ml/14fl oz semi-skimmed
    milk
1 medium cauliflower, cut into
    florets
1 large head of broccoli, cut into
    florets
2 tsp English mustard
salt and pepper
250g/8oz mature cheddar cheese,
    grated

Serves: 4 children + leftovers
Prep time: 10 minutes
Cooking time: 15 minutes

1 Start by bringing the steamer saucepan of water to the boil. Put the cauliflower and broccoli into different steamer tiers, as they cook at different speeds.

2 Gently fry the bacon. As soon as it is ready, blot it on some kitchen roll and put to one side.

3 In a medium saucepan, melt the butter. As it starts to bubble, add the flour and stir for a couple of minutes until the mixture starts to look a bit dry. Slowly pour on the milk, stirring all the time with the little whisk. Keep mixing until the sauce comes to the boil. Turn the heat down and simmer gently for 5 minutes.

4 Put the cauliflower on to steam on its own. After about 4 minutes, put the broccoli on above it. Steam both for a further 5 minutes.

5 Take the sauce off the heat and stir in the mustard and seasoning. Allow this to cool slightly before adding 200g/7oz of the cheese.

6 When the broccoli and cauliflower are cooked, place in a shallow dish and cover with the cheese sauce. Sprinkle the remaining cheese and place under a medium grill for about 7 minutes, until the cheese begins to brown.

7 Serve with the crispy fried bacon crumbled over the top.

chicken thighs with pasta, bacon and cherry tomatoes

I do find that anything with bacon is acceptable to children, and if you put bacon and chicken together you are onto a winner! This is fantastically easy and one of my regulars for when we all have supper as a family.

6 chicken thigh fillets
2 tbsp olive oil
140g/5oz pancetta cubes or bacon lardons
200ml/7fl oz white wine
300ml/11fl oz chicken stock (or half a chicken stock cube in hot water)
250g/8oz cherry tomatoes, halved
250g/8oz penne pasta
20 torn basil leaves

1 In a large, heavy-bottomed frying pan with a lid, brown the chicken thighs in the olive oil. When they have a good rich colour, add the pancetta and fry until the fat starts to run.

2 Turn up the heat and add the white wine, stirring to remove the crusty residue from the bottom of the pan. When the wine has reduced by about a third, add the chicken stock and bring back to the boil.

3 Turn the heat down to a simmer and tip the halved tomatoes into the pan, but don't stir them in.

4 Put the lid on and simmer gently for 20 minutes.

5 Meanwhile, place the pasta in a pan of boiling water and simmer for approximately 12 minutes. Drain and drizzle with a little olive oil.

Serves: 4 children
Prep time: 15 minutes
Cooking time: 35 minutes

6 Just before serving, add the torn basil to the chicken dish and gently stir.

7 Serve on a bed of pasta.

Tip

- This is a great way to get children to eat tomatoes. My youngest used to refuse until she saw how they soften when cooked, then suddenly they were acceptable and she now loves them. Sometimes you need to show children food in different ways just to break the habit they develop for disliking something.

cooking in
advance

One of the best tips my mother ever gave me when I had children was always to plan ahead – like me, Mum had four children very close in age, we lived on a farm and Mum pretty much single-handed looked after all the animals as well as us. She always swore by her time plan, and I remember we always had food on the table at the right time – never late! Often these were meals Mum had planned and started making the night before, or early in the morning before we had all woken up.

With the busy lifestyle that goes with having a young family, and the stress and tight schedule of working as well, dishes that you can prepare mostly in advance are vital – being able to walk in the front door knowing that you can pull a partially prepared homecooked meal out of the fridge is a real buzz, and eases the strain of having to start from scratch when children are demanding all your attention and you are tired, too!

slow-cooked lamb with apricots, ginger and cinnamon

The smell of this dish reminds me so much of coming home from school to find my mum by the stove in her apron with a large pot gently bubbling away ... I hope my children will remember the smells of my cooking favourably, too. Don't know about the apron, though!

1kg/2lb lamb, cut into pieces of
    approximately 2cm/1in
1 tbsp flour
4 tbsp olive oil
2cm/1in ginger, grated
2 cloves garlic, crushed
½ red chilli, seeds removed
3 spring onions
2 tbsp ground cumin
1 tsp ground coriander
1 tsp ground cinnamon
600ml/1 pint chicken stock
16 vine cherry tomatoes
4 sprigs thyme
12 dried apricots
6 pitted prunes, cut in half
    widthways
50g/2oz raisins
4 tbsp chopped fresh coriander
300g/10oz cous cous
25g/1oz flaked almonds

Serves: 4 hungry children
Prep time: 25 minutes
Cooking time: 2 hours

1   Preheat the oven to 160°C/310°F/GM2½.

2   Lightly roll the lamb in the flour. Fry the lamb in 2 tbsp of the oil. Remove with a slotted spoon. Add the ginger, garlic, chilli and spring onions to the pan and cook for around 2 minutes, until softened and like a paste. Add the spices and return the lamb to the pan. Stir in the stock, then put into an ovenproof dish and cook for 1 hour in the oven.

3   While the lamb is cooking, place the vine tomatoes on a baking sheet, drizzle over the remaining olive oil and add the sprigs of thyme. Roast in the oven for approximately half an hour. This really intensifies their natural flavour and complements the dish superbly.

4   Add the roasted cherry tomatoes, apricots, prunes and raisins and 2 tsp of the chopped coriander to the dish in the oven and cook for a further 30 minutes, or until ready to serve.

5   Cook the cous cous as directed on the packet. Lightly toast the flaked almonds in a small frying pan without oil. Dish up and cover with the lamb and sauce.

6   Just before serving sprinkle over the last of the chopped coriander and the flaked almonds.

red pepper and apple meatballs with sweet and sour sauce

A real classic - meatballs (with sneaky hidden goodies). These are best made either the night before and left in the fridge till tea time. This helps them not to fall apart while cooking.

For the meatballs
450g/1lb lean lamb mince
450g/1lb lean pork mince
1 red pepper, deseeded and finely
   chopped
1 small onion, finely chopped
3 Cox's apples, peeled and finely
   grated
1 tbsp grated ginger
4 tsp chopped coriander
1 egg white
flour
2 tsp olive oil

For the sauce
2 tsp olive oil
1 red onion, finely chopped
4 baby leeks, chopped
1 courgette, sliced
450g/1lb cherry tomatoes, halved
salt and pepper to season
2 tsp brown sugar (to taste)
2 tsp malt vinegar (to taste)
6 fresh basil leaves, torn

For the rice
300g/12oz Basmati rice

1   Place the pork and lamb mince into a large mixing bowl, and break it up a little. Add the finely chopped red pepper and onion, and then the grated apples, ginger and coriander. Add the egg white and mix all together.

2   Shape the mixture into small balls, approximately 2cm/1in in diameter, and place onto a tray lightly dusted with flour. Roll gently in the flour then place the tray in the fridge.

3   Meanwhile, in a medium frying pan heat up the olive oil and gently fry the onion until softened. Add the leeks and courgette and let them slightly colour, then add the halved tomatoes and let it all soften together. Check the seasoning, and add the brown sugar and malt vinegar. Let the sauce simmer gently.

4   After approximately 20 minutes place the sauce into the liquidizer and whizz until smooth.

5   Place back into the saucepan and leave aside.

6   Put the water on for the rice.

7 Heat up the 2 tsp of olive oil for the meatballs. I usually use two medium-sized deep frying pans for this. Get the tray of meatballs out of the fridge and, when the oil is nice and hot, place the meatballs in over a moderate heat, turning to ensure they are cooking evenly. After about 10 minutes ladle in the tomato sauce and allow this to heat thoroughly, until it is bubbling gently with the meatballs. Leave this to simmer for 15 minutes.

8 Drain and serve the rice, ladle on the meatballs and sauce. Garnish with basil and enjoy.

Serves: 4 (4 meatballs per child)
Prep time: 25 minutes
(refrigerate the meatballs once made)
Cooking time: 20 minutes

moroccan chicken with couscous

A naturally sweet dish, this is another one that I got from my mum - thank goodness for her endless stream of recipes. The only problem is my mum never ever cooks from a recipe as she has an amazing ability to always get quantities right just from touch and memory, so getting her to write it down for me was a mission! However, I have made this so many times I know these quantities are right.

2kg/4lb chicken (drumsticks and thighs)
2 large lemons
1 heaped tsp ground cinnamon
1 heaped tsp ground ginger
1 heaped tsp ground cumin
½ tsp cayenne pepper
pinch of salt – Maldon sea salt is best
1 large chopped onion
3 chopped garlic cloves
2 red peppers, deseeded and finely chopped
12 cherry tomatoes
500ml/1 pint chicken stock
15–20 stoned prunes
3 tbsp runny honey
250g/8oz couscous
Handful of lightly toasted almonds
2 tbsp chopped parsley

Serves: 6 people
Prep time: 25 minutes
Cooking time: 45 minutes

1 Start by preparing the chicken. Place the rind and juice of 1 lemon into the base of a large flat dish. Add the cinnamon, ginger, cumin and cayenne pepper and a little salt. Rub well into the chicken pieces, and marinate for as long as possible.

2 Heat up a little oil in a large saucepan and brown the chicken pieces. Take out and put aside. Gently fry the onion, garlic and red pepper. Add the tomatoes and the chicken stock and bring to just below the boil. Put the chicken back in the remaining marinade. Cover and simmer for approximately 20 minutes.

3 Add the stoned prunes and cook for another 15–20 minutes. Add the honey and 8 thin slices of lemon. Cook for a further 15–20 minutes.

4 Cook the couscous as directed on the packet, allowing 2oz per serving. Gently toast the almonds in a small frying pan with no oil.

5 Serve the chicken pieces onto the top of the couscous and generously ladle over the sauce. Sprinkle over chopped parsley and flaked almonds and serve.

stew and dumplings

This stew is all the proof needed that, with care and time, you don't need to spend a fortune to eat like a king.

400g/14oz carrots
400g/14oz parsnips
400g/14oz shallots
2 tbsp olive oil
450g/1lb diced stewing steak
1 tbsp plain flour
1 litre/2½ pints water
1 quality beef stock cube
1 tbsp malt vinegar
1 level dsp soft brown sugar
2 bay leaves
1 small bunch thyme, tied
salt and pepper

For the dumplings
175g/6oz self-raising flour
75g/3oz shredded suet
3 tbsp parsley, finely chopped
salt and pepper
water as needed

Serves: 6
Prep time: 30 minutes
Cooking time: 2½ hours

1 Preheat oven to 170°C/325°F/GM3.

2 Peel the carrots and parsnips and slice them diagonally into 2½cm/1in lengths. Peel the shallots.

3 Heat the oil in the casserole and add about a quarter of the beef to brown on a medium heat. When the meat is browned all over, remove and continue to brown the remainder in batches. By the time this process is complete, the bottom of the casserole should be covered in a layer of dark brown residue. This is essential to the flavour of the dish.

4 With the beef put to one side, add the carrots, parsnips and shallots and fry for about 5 minutes. You may need to add a little more olive oil. The vegetables should have a bit of colour to them, but not be burnt in any way.

5 Return the beef to the casserole. Sprinkle the flour all over the meat and stir together, lightly coating everything with the flour. Cook gently for about 3 minutes before adding the water. Gently stir while you bring the pan up to the boil, therefore preventing any nasty flour lumps forming. Reduce the heat and add the stock cube, vinegar, sugar and herbs. Season cautiously with salt and pepper.

6 Put the lid on the casserole and cook for 1½ hours. After 1½ hours, increase the temperature to 200°C/400°F/GM6 and cook for a further 30 minutes.

7 While the beef is cooking, make the dumpling mixture. Combine the flour, suet and parsley in a bowl and season well with salt and pepper. Then, very carefully, add enough water to form a smooth, elastic paste.

8 After the stew has cooked for 2 hours, take the casserole out of the oven. The stew will probably look fairly liquidy. This is absolutely fine – the dumplings will absorb a great deal of this excess liquid. Check the seasoning at this point. Dot the dumpling mixture all over. I make between 9 and 12 dumplings from these quantities, depending on how heavy-handed I am being!

9 Return the stew to the oven (without the lid) and cook for a further 30 minutes until the dumplings are crusty and golden.

10 Serve into bowls and enjoy!

chilli con carne

Chilli is the perfect girls'-night dinner - I make it in the afternoon so that it simmers slowly until it's ready to serve. That way I don't spend time at the stove when I have gossip to indulge in!

100g/3½oz sliced pancetta or
    bacon lardons
2 tbsp olive oil
85g/3oz butter
2 medium onions, peeled and
    finely chopped
2 cloves garlic, crushed
2 red chillies, deseeded and finely
    chopped
½ tsp chilli powder (optional)
2 small carrots, finely chopped
1kg/2lb beef mince
150ml/5 fl oz red wine
3 rounded tablespoons of tomato
    purée
1 tin kidney beans
300ml/½ pint fresh beef stock
Salt & pepper to season
350g/12oz basmati rice

1 Place the pancetta in a food processor and mince. Put in a pan along with the oil and ⅔ of the butter and brown lightly for approximately 5 minutes. Add the onions, garlic, chillies, chilli powder and the carrots. It becomes a little like a paste.

2 Cook over a low heat for about 10 minutes then add the beef mince and stir until browned and all broken up.

3 Add the wine and increase the heat slightly and cook for a further 10 minutes. Add the tomato purée, kidney beans and ⅔ of the stock. Bring to the boil, partially cover and simmer over a very low heat for approximately 1½ hours, or as long as possible – there should be gentle movement only. Stir occasionally. Add the remainder of the stock if necessary.

4 20 minutes before serving, heat the water for the rice and cook as directed. Drain when cooked and toss through the remaining butter.

Serves: 6 people
Prep time: 20 minutes
Cooking time: 1 hour 45 minutes
(but the longer the better)

Tip

• This is delicious served with mature cheddar grated on the top and a handful of tortilla chips!

ratatouille

This is fantastic cooked in autumn when the vegetables are in season and therefore much cheaper. The success of this dish depends on it not turning into one big brown mush of soggy vegetables. To make sure this doesn't happen, don't cut the vegetables up too small, and keep the temperature very low so they sweat rather than fry. I think this tastes better made the day before you need it.

4 tbsp olive oil
2 medium onions, quartered
2 cloves garlic
2 green peppers
2 red peppers
2 large aubergines, halved
   horizontally then sliced into
   2½cm/1in pieces
3 medium courgettes, sliced into
   2½cm/1in pieces
salt and pepper
400g/14oz tin chopped tomatoes,
   drained
1 small bunch basil

1 Heat the oil in a large casserole dish with a lid and sweat the onions and garlic for a good 10 minutes on a low heat, with the lid on.

2 Add the peppers, aubergines (I don't bother to salt the aubergines before using them, because I have never had a problem with bitterness, as long as I've used fresh ones) and courgettes, and season with salt and pepper.

3 Stir together carefully and put the casserole lid on. Allow to sweat for 30 minutes.

4 Add the tomatoes, check the seasoning and cook for a further 15 minutes without the lid.

5 Remove the leaves from the basil and tear them up a bit to allow the flavours to emerge. Add to the pan.

6 I think this is best served at room temperature with plenty of fresh brown bread. Serving it either too hot or too cold seems to dampen the various flavours.

Serves: 4
Prep time: 20 minutes
Cooking time: 1 hour

lamb shanks with balsamic vinegar and red wine

6 lamb shanks
plain flour for dusting, seasoned
2 tbsp olive oil
4 red onions, finely sliced
4 cloves garlic, sliced
170ml/6fl oz balsamic vinegar
310ml/11fl oz red wine
400g/14oz tin chopped tomatoes
1 tbsp rosemary, chopped
salt and pepper

1 Preheat oven to 170°C/325°F/GM3.

2 Dust the lamb shanks with the seasoned flour, shaking off any excess.

3 In the casserole, heat the oil and brown the shanks evenly. You may need to do this in batches, but as you finish each shank, remove to a nearby plate.

4 Lower the heat and add the onions. Cook for about 7 minutes, until soft and just starting to colour. Add the garlic and continue to cook for another couple of minutes.

5 Increase the heat slightly before adding the balsamic vinegar. As the vinegar is poured on to the onions, stir the bottom of the pan well to remove all the residue. Allow the vinegar to bubble away until it has reduced by about a half.

6 Return the shanks to the casserole and add the wine, tomatoes and rosemary. Season cautiously with salt and pepper.

7 Bring to the boil, put the lid on the casserole and place in the oven. Cook for about 2 hours until the meat falls off the bone easily.

8 Check seasoning before serving with a crisp, dark green salad and wholemeal bread.

Serves: 6
Prep time: 20 minutes
Cooking time: 2 hours

gammon with cloves

1.5kg/3½lb (approximately)
  unsmoked bacon joint
water as needed
3 medium onions, peeled and
  quartered
4 large carrots, cut into 2-cm/1-in
  chunks
2 celery stalks, halved
7 cloves
14 peppercorns
2 bay leaves
1 level dsp soft brown sugar
1 tbsp malt vinegar
8 floury potatoes, halved

For the parsley sauce
25g/1oz butter
25g/1oz plain flour
285g/½ pint semi-skimmed milk
3 tbsp parsley, finely chopped

Serves: 6
Prep time: 25 minutes
Cooking time: 1 hour 25 minutes
(based on 25 minutes per lb)

1 There seems to be a great debate on whether or not it is necessary to soak a bacon joint before cooking. Personally I feel happiest putting the joint in a large casserole of cold water, so that it is just covered, bringing it to the boil for a few minutes before discarding the water and continuing with the recipe. Maybe this is a waste of time, but it does away with removing the scum from what you want to be beautiful cooking liquor.

2 While you are bringing the bacon to the boil, prepare the onions, carrots and celery.

3 Once you have discarded the cooking water, rinse out the saucepan and return the bacon and vegetables to the pan, cover with boiling water and add the cloves, peppercorns, bay leaves, sugar and malt vinegar. Return to the boil and then simmer very gently with the lid on, for about 1 hour and 25 minutes.

4 To make the parsley sauce, melt the butter in a small saucepan and add the flour and mix together for a couple of minutes. Slowly pour on the milk and whisk constantly. Bring to the boil, stirring all the time, then let it simmer for about 5 minutes. If you don't want to use it straight away, put a disk of greaseproof paper on top of the sauce to prevent a skin forming. To use the sauce, bring it back to a simmer and stir in the parsley. Boil the potatoes until soft, drain and keep warm until needed.

5 Remove the bacon and vegetables from the casserole and discard the celery and bay leaves. With a slotted spoon, remove the carrots and onions to a warm serving dish.

6 Serve with broad beans, parsley sauce and some of the cooking liquor ladled over.

pork with apple and juniper berries

This is delicious served with baked potatoes, which are easy to put in the oven alongside the casserole 1 1/4 hours before you want to eat. It is also a great dish to make a day or two before you need it - it will keep brilliantly in the fridge while the flavours improve with time. This is very, very easy to prepare and cook, and makes a very satisfying winter supper.

1kg/2.2lb diced pork leg
2 tbsp olive oil
500ml/18fl oz sweet cider
200ml/7fl oz water + ½ chicken
    stock cube
1 tbsp rosemary, finely chopped
1 tbsp juniper berries
2 Bramley apples
115ml/4fl oz crème fraîche
25g/1oz butter

Serves: 4
Prep time: 25 minutes
Cooking time: 2 hours

1 Preheat oven to 170°C/325°F/GM3.

2 Start by browning the meat in batches in a large casserole dish with a lid. As each batch is ready, remove to a waiting plate.

3 When all the meat has been well browned (it is important to brown the pork well, otherwise the finished dish will look rather insipid), return to the pan and pour over the cider, stirring well to incorporate all the residue on the bottom of the pan.

4 Add the stock, rosemary, juniper berries and apples.

5 Make sure you bring the liquid to the boil before placing the lid on the casserole and putting in the oven.

6 Cook for 1½ hours but check occasionally to make sure the liquid hasn't evaporated too much. Check that the meat is tender before serving. Stir in crème fraîche and butter, and serve with well-buttered baked potatoes.

fish pie

An important dish to have in any household! You can hide all sorts of
vegetables in this pie, although it is nice to keep it simple as well. Vary the
ingredients as you wish!

300g/10oz cod, skinless and
    boneless
300g/10oz salmon fillet, skinless
    and boneless
400ml/¾ pint milk
    (to cover the fish to poach)
1 large onion, finely chopped
6 baby leeks, finely sliced
1 tbsp olive oil
5 large potatoes
2 tbsp double cream
knob of butter
salt and pepper to season
4 tbsp Cheddar cheese
    (to sprinkle on the top)

For the white sauce
45g/1½ oz butter
45g/1½ oz flour
450ml/¾ pint full fat milk

Serves: 4 children
Prep time: 20 minutes
Cooking time: 20 minutes

1 Preheat oven to 190ºC/375ºF/GM5.

2 Place the fish in a frying pan and cover with
   the milk to poach. This takes approximately
   10 minutes.

3 Fry the onion and the leeks in a little olive oil
   until softened. Flake the fish into the onion and
   leeks and mix gently together.

4 Peel and cut the potatoes into large chunks
   and put on to boil. Meanwhile, make the white
   sauce. Melt the butter in a small saucepan. Stir
   in the flour, mixing to a paste, then stir over the
   heat for a minute or two, taking care not to let
   it catch on the bottom. Add the milk gradually,
   and whisk constantly until it starts to simmer.
   Leave it to cook over a very low heat, stirring
   every couple of minutes until it thickens.

5 Mix the white sauce with the fish, onion and
   leeks and place this mixture into the bottom of
   an ovenproof dish.

6 Check the potatoes and, if tender, drain and
   place back into the saucepan to mash. Add the
   cream and a knob of butter, season and mash.

7 Spoon the mash over the top of the fish and
   vegetables and sprinkle with the cheese.

8 Put in the oven for approximately 15 minutes,
   until bubbling.

9 Place under the grill for a couple of minutes to
   crisp and brown the top, then serve.

bolognaise

I know that there are a-million-and-one different recipes for bolognaise sauce, but I think it is a really useful way of hiding loads of vegetables. Consequently my recipe tries to include as many as possible! Although spaghetti and children is a very messy combination, the enthusiasm with which my children eat a bowl of pasta makes cleaning up the mess worthwhile. The quantities here are large, but it freezes well and I always know that there is a healthy and popular standby supper in the freezer for emergencies.

2 tbsp olive oil
150g/5oz pancetta, cubed
  (or unsmoked streaky bacon)
2 medium onions, finely chopped
2 garlic cloves, crushed
2 carrots, diced
2 stalks celery, diced
1 courgette, diced
100g/4oz mushrooms, diced
500g/1lb extra lean beef mince
200ml/7fl oz red wine
400g/14oz tin chopped tomatoes
200ml/7fl oz water + ½ quality
  beef stock cube
2 bay leaves
salt and pepper
parmesan (optional)

Serves: 4 children, three times
Prep time: 30 minutes
Cooking time: 2 hours

1 Heat the oil in the pan before adding the pancetta. Cook until it is just beginning to colour and crisp around the edges.

2 Add the onions and garlic and stir together. Cook for about 5 minutes before adding the carrots, celery, courgette and mushrooms. Allow to cook together for about 10 minutes on a relatively low heat.

3 Turn the heat up and add the beef mince. Keep stirring it to break the clumps up and mix thoroughly with the vegetables. When the mince is completely incorporated, cook for a further 5 minutes without stirring, to allow the bottom of the pan to start browning.

4 Pour over the wine and scrape the bottom of the pan in order to remove the residue from the bottom. Allow the wine to reduce by about a half before adding the tinned tomatoes and stock. Tuck in the bay leaves and season with a little salt and a good grinding of pepper.

5 Bring to the boil before reducing the heat until it barely bubbles. Put the lid on and leave to simmer, very gently, for 2 hours. During the cooking time, check the liquid levels several times just to make sure it is not boiling dry. If necessary, add a little boiling water.

6 Before serving, check the seasoning and if necessary add a little more salt. Serve with plenty of grated parmesan and wholemeal spaghetti.

Tip

- Make sure the bolognaise has completely cooled before placing the airtight containers in the freezer.

cassoulet

Cassoulet (illustrated overleaf) requires a great deal of meat, making it rather expensive. However, as a treat on a very cold day it's great for the soul.

500g/18oz dried haricot beans
500g/18oz Toulouse sausage
(or English garlic and herb
alternative)
2 duck breasts (with skin)
500g/18oz stewing pork, diced
350g/12oz lamb neck fillet
(approximately 2), diced
400g/14oz shallots
250g/8oz pancetta, cubed, or
bacon lardons
1 litre/2½ pints chicken stock
small bunch of rosemary and
thyme, tied together
3 bay leaves
3 tbsp flat leaf parsley, coarsely
chopped
salt and pepper
1 jar duck confit (optional)

1 You need to think ahead a little before starting this recipe. The day before you intend to make the cassoulet, place the dried haricot beans in a large bowl of water and leave to soak overnight. The following morning, drain the beans and put in a large saucepan; cover with fresh water. Bring to the boil and simmer for 1 hour. Drain and put to one side until you are ready for them.

2 Preheat oven to 200°C/400°F/GM6.

3 Put the Toulouse sausages in the oven for 20 minutes to brown, but not cook through completely. As soon as they are browned, reduce the heat to 170°C/325°F/GM3.

4 Meanwhile, remove the fatty skin from the duck breast. Heat a large casserole dish with a lid on the hob and carefully put the duck skin into it. An amazing amount of fat will run from the skin. When there is enough fat to cover the bottom of the casserole, remove the duck skins and discard. Using this fat, brown the pork and lamb in small batches. Place to one side.

5   Still using the casserole, fry the shallots and
    pancetta together until they are beginning
    to colour.

6   Add the beans, all the meat, stock, herbs,
    pepper and a cautious seasoning of salt.

7   Bring to the boil before placing in the oven
    for 2 hours.

8   After 2 hours, add the sausages and duck
    confit, if you are using this. Check the moisture
    levels and top up with some boiling water if
    necessary. Cook for a further hour.

9   Serve with plenty of warm, crusty granary
    bread and (adults only!) lashings of good
    red wine.

Serves: 10
Prep time: 25 minutes
Cooking time: 3 hours

Tip

- This tastes really wonderful if you cook it up to two
  days in advance. When I do this, I prepare everything up until the point in the recipe where I
  add the sausages and duck confit. At this stage I allow the cassoulet to cool and then
  refrigerate until I need it. Warm the cassoulet through on the hob before adding the sausages
  and duck confit. Then continue with the recipe as above.

- Duck confit is quite hard to get, so you can substitute it with 250ml/9fl oz each of olive oil and
  vegetable oil, a clove of crushed garlic, a small bunch of thyme and 2 sprigs of rosemary.

This cassoulet is the ultimate winter indulgence.

mutton daube

Although not currently available in supermarkets, some butchers stock mutton. Cook the day before to allow all the flavours to develop.

For the marinade
2kg/4.4lb boned shoulder of mutton
2 onions, sliced
4 carrots, sliced
small bunch of thyme
2 bay leaves
4 cloves garlic, crushed but whole
pepper
1 bottle red wine

For the Daube
4 tbsp olive oil
400g/14oz shallots
250g/8oz pancetta, cubed, or bacon lardons
2 garlic cloves, crushed
400g/14oz tin chopped tomatoes
500ml/18fl oz water with quality lamb stock cube
2 tbsp parsley, chopped

Serves: 8
Prep time: 30 minutes
Cooking time: 2½–3 hours

1 The day before you are due to cook the Daube (two days before you want to eat it), marinade the mutton in the marinade ingredients. Leave in the fridge overnight.

2 Preheat the oven to 170°C/325°F/GM3.

3 Remove the mutton from the marinade and place to one side. Drain the remaining marinade ingredients but keep the liquid.

4 Heat the oil in a large casserole and brown the mutton on all sides in batches. Place on a plate.

5 Fry the shallots and pancetta in the casserole until golden. Add the garlic and cook for a couple of minutes. Return the mutton to the casserole and mix.

6 Pour on the marinade liquid and turn up the heat; allow to reduce by about half.

7 Add the tomatoes and stock and bring to the boil. Place the lid on the casserole and place in the oven for 2½ to 3 hours. Every hour, check the fluid levels of the Daube and if necessary add more boiling water.

8 When tender, remove the mutton from the oven and allow to cool. Place in the fridge overnight.

9 When you remove the casserole from the fridge, take off all the hardened fat from the surface before, very gently, bringing to the boil. Allow to simmer for 20 minutes, making sure everything is piping hot before serving.

10 Sprinkle with chopped parsley and serve.

weekend lunches

There is nothing quite like the weekend when you get real family time. There is no timetable to adhere to like on weekdays, and mealtimes can be a little more indulgent and leisurely. It is just as important for meals at this time to be as attractive to adults as to children, and you want food that is easy to cook for larger numbers.

minestrone

This is a recipe Gordon wrote out for me after cooking it one evening for the children. It was so delicious that I often make it for tea on a Saturday night, especially in the winter when the kids have been out cycling and come in freezing cold - they can have it in a mug and warm their hands on it while spooning out the chunky bits.

1 large red onion, peeled and
   finely chopped
1 clove of garlic, crushed
1 tsp fresh rosemary
2 tbsp olive oil
250g/10oz pancetta cubes or
   bacon lardons
1 carrot, peeled and finely chopped
1 small swede, peeled and diced
2 sticks of celery, finely sliced
1 leek, finely chopped
salt and pepper
1 tbsp tomato purée
2 litres/3½ pints vegetable stock
100g/4oz spaghetti
½ Savoy cabbage, roughly chopped
250g/10oz mangetouts, halved
15 cherry tomatoes, halved
handful of fresh basil, torn

Makes: 6 bowls or 12 mugs
Prep time: 10 minutes
Cooking time: 45 minutes

1 Fry the onion, garlic and rosemary in the olive oil in a large frying pan until they start to soften. Add the pancetta cubes and once they start to colour, add the carrot, swede, celery and leek, cooking for 2–3 minutes till they soften. Add a pinch of salt and a couple of twists of black pepper and the tomato purée. Continue to stir, then when the purée starts to lose its colour, add the vegetable stock. Turn the heat down to a simmer and let it continue cooking for about 20 minutes.

2 Add the spaghetti to the soup, breaking it up into pieces of approximately 1½ inches, and continue to simmer the soup until the pasta is ready, approximately 10–12 minutes. Lastly, add the cabbage, mangetouts, and cherry tomatoes and cook for a further 5 minutes. Check the seasoning and serve with basil scattered on the surface.

Tips

• This is great served with crusty white rolls and butter.

• Extra tasty served with a spoonful of basil pesto (recipe on page 121).

new york sandwich

This is the ultimate weekend sandwich if you just want a light bite.

For the balsamic onion marmalade
2 tbsp grapeseed oil
700g/1lb 12oz red onions, thinly sliced
1 tsp salt
1 tsp pepper
150g/6oz caster sugar
10 tbsp balsamic vinegar
250ml/9fl oz red wine

For the sandwich
cold rare roast beef, sliced thinly (allow approximately 4oz per sandwich)
2tbsp horseradish sauce
2 ciabatta rolls

Serves: 2
Prep time: 15 minutes
Cooking time: 20 minutes

1 Heat the grapeseed oil in a saucepan until it shimmers. Add the onions, salt, pepper and caster sugar. Cook very slowly for about 40 minutes until the onions have caramelized.

2 Add the vinegar and red wine and bring to the boil. Simmer for a further 30 minutes, stirring occasionally, until the liquid has reduced to a marmalade-like consistency.

3 Allow to cool, check the seasonings and pour into jam jars. Cool thoroughly before putting in the fridge. It will keep for a month or so very happily.

4 To make the sandwich, make sure the beef and marmalade are at room temperature and the roll is warm and fresh. Make sure you are generous with your quantities – scrimping on any of the ingredients will ruin the experience!

chicken in a pot

This is so easy to make, but real family comfort food. I serve it with floury boiled potatoes sprinkled with lots of chopped parsley.

2 tbsp olive oil
150g/6oz unsmoked streaky
   bacon, cut into 1cm slices
400g/15oz shallots, peeled
2kg/4.4lb free-range chicken
3 medium carrots, cut into 2cm
   chunks
3 medium leeks, cut into 2cm
   slices
250ml/9fl oz white wine
500ml/18fl oz chicken stock
400ml/14oz tin chopped tomatoes
1 tbsp fresh thyme leaves,
   chopped
3 bay leaves
200g/8oz button mushrooms
1 tbsp plain flour
25g/1oz butter

To serve with
6 floury potatoes
6 tsp fresh parsley, finely chopped
loads of butter for each potato!

1 Preheat oven to 200°C/400°F/GM6.

2 Begin by heating the olive oil in the casserole and frying the bacon and shallots until just colouring. Remove them to a nearby plate and put to one side.

3 Place the chicken in the casserole and brown on all sides, taking care as you turn it over as the hot fat may spit. When it has a good golden colour all over, take out and put to one side.

4 Put the carrots and leeks in the casserole and fry for about 5 minutes before returning the chicken, bacon and shallots to the pot.

5 Pour over the wine, chicken stock and chopped tomatoes. Mix in the chopped thyme and bay leaves, making sure they are pushed under the surface of the liquid.

6 Bring to the boil before putting on the lid and placing in the oven for 30 minutes. It is important that the lid is a very close-fitting one. If in doubt, take a piece of greaseproof paper or baking parchment that is about 10cm wider than the casserole, scrunch it up and dampen with water. Put over the chicken with the lid on top; this will help to make the casserole more airtight.

7 After 30 minutes, baste the chicken well and add the button mushrooms. Return to the oven without the lid for a further 30 minutes.

8 Make a paste with the flour and butter and set to one side. If serving with potatoes put these on now to boil.

9 After the cooking time has finished, put the chicken on a serving plate, turn the oven temperature off, and return the chicken on its plate to the oven with the door ajar while you make the gravy.

10 Using a slotted spoon, remove all the vegetables from the pot and put in a warm serving dish.

11 Keeping the casserole over a moderate heat, stir the flour-and-butter paste into the juices. Keep stirring until it comes to the boil. Allow to simmer for 2 minutes, during which time you can get the chicken from the oven and start carving.

12 Serve with the cooked vegetables and potatoes, sprinkled with parsley and loads of butter.

Serves: 6 (or 4 if very hungry!)
Prep time: 20 minutes
Cooking time: 1 hour 15 minutes

steak burgers with roasted red pepper sauce

For the roasted red pepper sauce

4 red peppers, quartered and
  de-seeded
2 cloves garlic, crushed
salt and pepper
1 tbsp extra-virgin olive oil

For the burgers

500g/1lb minced steak
1 red onion, finely diced
1 medium red chilli, finely
  chopped
salt and pepper
6 good-quality soft rolls
  (I use ciabatta rolls)
1 tbsp olive oil

1   Begin by making the red pepper sauce. Take the peppers and place, skin-side up, on a baking tin. Put under a hot grill until the skins are completely blackened. Put the pieces of pepper in a sandwich bag and, as quickly as possible, knot it to keep the steam and heat in. Leave to cool and, when you can handle them easily, slip off the burnt skin and place the cooked flesh in a food processor.

2   Add the garlic and a good pinch of salt and plenty of pepper. Blitz in the mixer until smooth. With the motor running, gradually pour in the olive oil.

3   To make the burgers, mix the minced steak, onion, chilli, salt and pepper together in a bowl. Divide the mixture into 6 portions and gently squeeze into patty shapes using your hands.

4   Heat the grill to a fairly high setting and cut the soft rolls in half. Place on a baking tray, cut sides up, and put to one side.

5   Heat a large frying pan until it is very hot. Add the olive oil and, as it starts to shimmer, carefully place the burger patties into the pan.

6   Cook for 3 minutes on each side before reducing the temperature to low.

7   Put the rolls under the grill and remove as soon as they start to brown and crisp. Place a burger in each one and serve with plenty of roasted red pepper sauce and a watercress salad.

Serves: 6
Prep time: 20 minutes
Cooking time: 15 minutes

Tip

• You can make the sauce up to four days in advance and keep in a sealed container in the fridge.

osso bucco

My mum used to do this dish for Saturday lunches - I always remember a noisy lunch table, lots of red wine for the adults and squash for us. The delicacy is the bone marrow - some people love it, some don't.

6 veal pieces – specify 'osso bucco'
flour to coat (approx 2 tsp per
   piece, so 12 tsp)
2 tbsp olive oil
knob of butter
3 white onions, finely chopped
3 large sticks of celery, finely
   chopped
3 large carrots, finely chopped
2 cloves garlic, crushed
4 pieces lemon peel (shaved)
3 bay leaves
1 tsp dried thyme
salt and pepper
705ml/1¼ pints of stock
   (I use chicken stock)
425ml/¾ pint white wine
1 tube tomato purée
zest of another lemon
2 tbsp flat parsley, chopped
4 cups/12oz Basmati rice

Serves: 6
Prep time: 20 minutes
Cooking time: 3 hours (not all hands on, some is slow cooking time!)

1 Coat the veal pieces in flour and brown in a casserole dish in the oil and butter.

2 Remove the veal from the dish and put in the onions, celery, carrots and garlic. Cook until soft, not crisp. Put the veal on the top of these and add the lemon peel, bay leaves and thyme. Add two pinches of Maldon salt and a couple of twists of black pepper.

3 Mix together the stock and the wine and the tomato purée and put into the casserole dish. Bring this all to the boil, cover and simmer on a very low heat (so there is movement but it is not bubbling) for 2–2½ hours.

4 Take out the veal and keep it warm. Turn up the heat to reduce the sauce – this is really to your taste; I like it fairly thick and a dark consistency. At this point boil the water for the rice and cook as directed. When the sauce is to your taste, turn down the heat and stir in the lemon zest and parsley. Put the veal back in and stir it gently to coat it and ensure it is hot throughout.

5 Serve a shin per person on a bed of rice.

roast rib of beef

I think the secret, if there is one, to a successful roast lunch is making sure you have a notebook and pen nearby in order to write a very rudimentary timetable of events. Mine usually consists of three columns: one for the meat, one for the roast potatoes, and one for the Yorkshire pudding. The first thing to do is to write at the bottom of each column the time you are planning to eat, and from that work backwards. I'm usually about 10 minutes later than I intended, but nobody seems to mind!

2½kg/5½lb rib of beef
1 medium onion, peeled and
   halved
1 dsp plain flour
1 dsp dry mustard
pepper

For the Yorkshire pudding
170g/6oz plain flour
3 large eggs
425ml/15fl oz whole milk
good pinch of salt

For the gravy
1 tbsp plain flour
200ml/7fl oz red wine
300ml/11fl oz beef stock or water

1 Remove the beef from the fridge and all its packaging about 2 hours before you intend to start cooking.

2 Place on a wire roasting rack, fat uppermost, above a baking tray with the halved onion underneath.

3 Set the oven to 220°C/435°F/GM7½.

4 Mix together the flour, mustard and pepper and sprinkle over the beef fat.

5 Place the beef in the oven and roast for 20 minutes.

6 After the 20 minutes has elapsed, turn the oven down to 160°C/310°F/GM2½ and continue cooking for a further 1 hour and 40 minutes.

7 While the beef is cooking, make the Yorkshire pudding batter. Simply put all the ingredients into the liquidizer goblet and blend until smooth. You may need to stop the motor and scrape down the sides of the goblet in order to incorporate all the flour into the mixture. Put to one side until needed.

8 At the end of the cooking time, remove the beef from the oven and put on a warm serving dish. Cover with tin foil and put in a warm place to rest for 30 minutes.

9 Put the Yorkshire pudding tray into the oven and increase the oven temperature to 200°C/400°F/GM6 as you remove the beef from the oven. As the fat in the pudding tray begins to smoke, add the batter and put in the oven. Make sure you don't open the oven door for the next 15 minutes, or the puddings won't rise well. When they are golden and risen, take them out of the oven and turn each pudding upside down before returning to the oven for another couple of minutes before serving.

10 As soon as the beef is on the serving plate, start to make the gravy. Pour most of the beef dripping out of the pan, taking care to leave the brown juices and onion behind. Add the flour to the remaining fat and juices and stir over the heat until the flour has browned and any sediment from the bottom of the pan is loosened. Add the red wine and stir until there are no lumps. Add the beef stock and continue to simmer for 5 minutes. Pass the gravy through a sieve to remove the onion.

Serves: 8
Prep time: 20 minutes
Cooking time: 2½ hours

moussaka

A well-made moussaka is a fantastic dish - it's not hard to make and freezes particularly well. This is a recipe that my sister Olly regularly makes and says it is the easiest and the best one she has used - she should know, she got a better grade than I did at home economics, as she constantly reminds me! And, I grudgingly add, my children love her cooking and whenever we go to her house clean their plates at twice the usual speed.

3 large aubergines, sliced to
   approx 1cm thick
2 tbsp pure olive oil
3 large onions
4 cloves of garlic, crushed
1 tsp ground cinnamon
1 tsp dried marjoram
3 tbsp tomato purée
140g/5oz pancetta or bacon lardons
500g/1lb lean minced lamb
400ml/14fl oz red wine
300ml chicken stock
salt and pepper to season
2 tbsp flat leaf parsley, chopped

For the béchamel sauce
450ml/¾ pint milk
2 small onions, finely chopped
2 bay leaves
pinch of salt
1 tsp Dijon mustard
45g/1½oz butter
45g/1½oz flour
nutmeg, freshly grated
150g/6oz parmesan cheese, grated

1 Preheat oven to 190°C/375°F/GM5.

2 Brush the aubergines lightly with a little of the olive oil and place under the grill until they become slightly golden. Repeat on the other side and with all the slices. Place to one side.

3 In a large frying pan, gently fry the onions and garlic in the olive oil until softened. Add the cinnamon and the marjoram, then stir through tomato purée, allowing all to become a mushy paste. Add the pancetta and the lamb, breaking it up and frying gently till a little brown. Remove the pan and tip the lamb and pancetta into a colander to remove the excess fat. Return to the pan. Add the red wine and stock and season with salt and pepper.

4 Allow this all to simmer gently for approximately 45 minutes. There should be movement but no bubbling.

5 While the lamb mince is simmering, start to make your béchamel sauce.

6   Put the milk, onions, bay leaves, salt and mustard into a small sauce pan. Bring this to a medium heat, cover and allow to infuse for approximately 15 minutes. When this is done, pour through a sieve into a jug. Discard the onions and bay leaves.

7   Melt the butter gently and mix in the flour, forming a paste, but constantly stirring so that it does not stick. Add the milk from the jug slowly and, using a whisk, whisk constantly and let the sauce begin to simmer. Let the sauce continue to cook, stirring at 1-minute intervals for 3–4 minutes.

8   Add the nutmeg and the parmesan cheese and stir over the heat until the cheese has melted and the sauce has thickened. Keep warm and cover with a lid/tin foil.

9   Meanwhile, sprinkle the flat leaf parsley into the lamb mince, add a little more black pepper and stir through.

10 Line the bottom of the ovenproof dish with half of the aubergine slices, then using a slotted spoon, spoon over the lamb mince. Cover this with the other half of the aubergine slices, then spoon over the béchamel sauce.

11 Place the dish in the oven and cook for 25–30 minutes, until the top is bubbling and starting to brown in areas.

12 Serve immediately, or allow to cool completely and freeze.

Serves: 8
Prep time: 30 minutes
Cooking time: 1 hour 30 minutes

paella with chicken and prawns

No two paella dishes taste the same, so there is a great deal of room to adapt this basic recipe and turn it into your own family classic. Paella rice is now widely available in supermarkets, and I think it makes a big difference to use it rather than long grain or basmati rice.

6 tbsp olive oil
350g/12oz chicken breast,
    cut into 2cm cubes
3 medium onions, finely chopped
85g/3oz bacon, diced
1 red pepper, finely chopped
1 green pepper, finely chopped
3 garlic cloves, crushed
150g/6oz green beans, top,
    tailed and halved
1 tsp paprika
250g/10oz paella rice
salt and pepper
1 litre/1½ pints chicken stock,
    heated
1 pinch saffron
75ml/2½fl oz white wine
400g/14oz large uncooked prawns
    (without shells)
1 lemon, quartered

1 Begin by heating 2 tablespoons of oil in a pan over a medium heat. As the oil begins to smoke, add the pieces of chicken and stir-fry for about 3 minutes until they are sealed on all sides, but not completely cooked.

2 Remove with a slotted spoon and put to one side.

3 Add the remaining olive oil and fry the onions and bacon. After about 5 minutes, add the red and green peppers and continue to fry, stirring all the time, for another 5 minutes.

4 Reduce the heat and continue to cook for a further 10 minutes, stirring occasionally.

5 Add the garlic, beans and paprika and cook for another 5 minutes.

6 Add the rice to the pan and stir for a minute or so, until all the vegetables are coated with rice. Season well with salt and pepper.

7 In another saucepan, bring the chicken stock and saffron to the boil.

8 Put the paella pan on a medium to high heat and add the white wine and hot stock. It is very important that from this moment onwards you resist any temptation to stir the paella. Unlike a risotto, paella will be completely ruined if you stir it while the rice is cooking and absorbing the liquid.

9 Simmer for 10 minutes or until there is just a little liquid above the rice. Spread the chicken pieces evenly over the rice and, with the back of a spoon, push each piece down underneath the stock. Gently shake the pan to prevent anything from sticking, reduce the temperature to low and leave to cook for a further 5 minutes.

10 Arrange the prawns over the top of the paella, turn off the heat and cover the pan tightly with tin foil.

11 Leave for 10 minutes before serving with pieces of lemon and a large green salad and bread.

Serves: 4
Prep time: 20 minutes
Cooking time: 30 minutes

leek and bacon pie

This is a favourite for my children; they love the crispy potatoes topped with cheesy sauce, and the way the top is slightly crunchy.

For the topping
4 large potatoes

For the cheese sauce
45g/1½oz butter
45g/1½oz flour
450ml/¾ pint milk
2 tsp grain mustard
    (Poupon is best)
150g/6oz mature cheddar cheese,
    grated

For the filling
2 tbsp butter
200g/8oz streaky bacon, rind
    removed
1kg/2lb leeks trimmed and finely
    sliced into 1cm thick slices
100g/4oz sliced button
    mushrooms
45g/1½oz flour
570ml/1 pint stock
1 lemon, juice and zest
½ tsp grated nutmeg
salt and pepper

Serves: 8
Prep time: 20 minutes
Cooking time: 35 minutes

1 Preheat oven to 190°C/375°F/GM5.

2 Peel the potatoes and parboil them in lightly salted water for approximately 10 minutes. Tip them into a colander and allow to cool. When cooled, slice them thinly (approximately ½cm thick) and leave aside.

3 For the cheese sauce, melt the butter and stir in the flour, mixing to a paste. Stir over the heat for a minute or two, taking care not to let it catch on the bottom. Add the milk and whisk constantly until it starts to simmer. Leave it to cook over a very low heat, stirring occasionally. Add the mustard and stir in the cheese; continue to cook and stir until the cheese has melted and the sauce becomes thick and creamy. Cover the saucepan with a lid and leave aside until ready to use.

4 Melt the butter in a large pan, add the bacon and fry gently for 3 minutes. Add the leeks and mushrooms, and continue frying until they are soft, but not brown. Add the flour fry for a further minute or two, add the stock and lemon juice and zest. Bring to the boil, lower the heat and simmer until the sauce is thick and smooth, stirring constantly. Season and add nutmeg.

5 Tip the filling into an ovenproof dish. Layer the potato on top, then pour over the cheese sauce. Place in the oven and cook for 25–30 minutes. The top should be bubbling and slightly crispy. For the final 5 minutes, place under the grill to get the top nice and crispy.

steak and guinness pie

Serve with boiled new potatoes or homemade chunky chips (see page 126) for an authentic pub grub dish at home!

2 tbsp olive oil
3 medium onions, sliced
200g/8oz button mushrooms
1½kg/3.3lb lean braising steak,
    cubed
2 tbsp plain flour
350ml/12fl oz Guinness
350ml/12fl oz beef stock
100g/4oz Stilton
salt and pepper
½ x 500g/1lb pack puff pastry
25g/1oz butter, melted

1　Heat the olive oil in the saucepan and add the sliced onions and button mushrooms. Put the lid on the saucepan and leave to sweat over a low heat for about 10 minutes.

2　When the onions and mushrooms have softened, remove from the saucepan and put to one side.

3　Turn the heat up and brown the braising steak all over. You will need to do this in several batches, so have a plate nearby for the already browned meat.

4　When all the meat is ready, return to the saucepan. Sprinkle over the flour and stir for 2 minutes until the flour has coated all the meat and absorbed the fat in the pan.

5　Carefully pour on the Guinness and stock and bring to the boil, stirring all the time. Return the mushrooms and onions to the saucepan, replace the lid and simmer gently for 1 hour.

6　After an hour, remove the lid and simmer for a further 40 minutes to 1 hour, allowing some of the liquid to evaporate. After 40 minutes, check to see how tender the meat is. It should not be at all chewy. If it is, continue to cook for another 20 minutes.

7 Crumble the Stilton (including the rind) into the meat and, over a low heat, stir well until it has melted. Continue to cook for a further 5 minutes, stirring all the time.

8 Remove from the heat and check the seasoning.

9 Heat oven to 200ºC/400ºF/GM6.

10 On a lightly floured surface, roll the pastry to the thickness of about 5mm. Turn the pie dish upside down and, using it as a template, cut around the rim with a sharp knife allowing an extra 2.5cm around the edge of the dish. This will allow you to stick the pastry to the rim of the pie dish.

11 Transfer the meat mixture to the pie dish. Wet the rim of the dish with a little water and place the pastry on top, gently pressing the edges to the rim to seal it down.

12 Using the blunt edge of a knife, gently push back the pastry around the edge of the rim using your thumb's width as an approximate measure of the distance between each knife strike.

13 Carefully brush the pastry lid with melted butter before placing the completed dish on a baking sheet in the oven for about 20 minutes, until the pastry is golden brown.

Serves: 6
Prep time: 20 minutes
Cooking time: approximately 2½ hours (some is simmering time)

chicken and mango casserole

2kg/4.4lb chicken thighs –
  skinless and boneless
2 tbsp olive oil
2 tbsp butter
1 large onion
1 mango, peeled and diced
1 tsp lemon zest, grated
½ tsp ground coriander
½ tsp ground cinnamon
250ml/9fl oz chicken stock
250ml/9fl oz single cream
2 tsp flour
1 tbsp lemon juice
1 tbsp water
4 cups/12oz plain rice

Serves: 6
Prep time: 25 minutes
Cooking time: 2 hours (again, not all
hands on, some is simmering time)

1 Preheat oven to 190°C/375°F/GM5.

2 Brown the chicken pieces in a large frying
   pan with the oil and butter, then transfer to a
   casserole dish. Fry the onion until soft then
   put it in with the chicken pieces.

3 Add the mango pieces to the frying pan,
   gently fry them over a lower heat, turning
   them carefully. This takes approximately
   4 minutes. Stir in the lemon zest, coriander,
   cinnamon and chicken stock. Bring this mix
   to the boil, then pour all into the casserole
   dish. Cover this dish and bake for 1½ hours.
   Remove from the oven.

4 Take out the chicken pieces and keep warm.
   Turn up the heat on the hob and bring the
   liquid to the boil, let it reduce down and
   thicken, then turn down the heat a little and
   stir through the cream. Put the rice on and
   cook as directed. Mix together the flour,
   lemon juice and water and beat this into the
   sauce. Let it all simmer together for a further
   15 minutes, then return the chicken pieces,
   mix through, ensure the chicken is hot
   throughout and serve over a bed of rice.

calves' liver with bacon

This is a very quick and straightforward way of cooking liver. It requires very little preparation, but does call for very good-quality, fresh liver.

8 slices thinly sliced pancetta or unsmoked streaky bacon
300g/12oz cherry tomatoes on the vine
450g/1lb calves' liver, thinly sliced
flour – enough to dust the liver, seasoned with a little salt and pepper
100g/4oz butter
100ml/4fl oz Marsala wine

Serves: 4
Prep time: 10 minutes
Cooking time: 10 minutes

1 Preheat oven to 180°C/350°F/GM4.

2 Start by laying the slices of pancetta between two pieces of baking parchment and placing on a baking sheet.

3 Put a smaller baking tin on top of the pancetta, effectively weighing it down. Inside the second baking tin, place the tomatoes. Cut the stems so that you have about four bunches of tomatoes with about five tomatoes on each bunch.

4 Put in the oven and cook for 5 minutes. Remove the pancetta but continue cooking the tomatoes for a further 10 minutes.

5 Dry the liver thoroughly between pieces of kitchen paper before dusting with seasoned flour. Put to one side carefully, keeping the pieces of liver apart.

6 If you can, use two frying pans. Otherwise have a warm plate waiting and fry the liver in batches.

7 On a fairly high heat, melt 1oz of butter in each of the two frying pans and, as it starts to foam, carefully add the liver. Fry the liver for about 2 minutes, or until you see blood coming from the top of the liver.

8 Flip over and fry for another 2 minutes. Any longer and it will become tough. The idea is to have the liver brown on the outside but pale pink on the inside.

9 Remove the liver to warm serving plates and, keeping the frying pans on a high heat, pour in the Marsala. Be careful because it will spit. Add the remaining butter to the bubbling Marsala and allow to boil.

10 In the meantime, put two rashers of pancetta and a bunch of tomatoes on each portion of liver.

11 By this time the bubbling Marsala will have reduced by about a half. Spoon about 1 tablespoon of the liquid over each portion of liver and serve with a watercress salad and warm, crusty brown bread.

aromatic lamb burgers

Perfect for a romantic lunch for two with a bottle of chilled white wine and the children safely packed off to their grandparents! For the ultimate indulgence, serve with chunky chips (see page 126) and a mixed salad.

For the burgers
225g/8oz lamb mince
30g/1oz bread crumbs (1 slice of stale bread whizzed in the food processor)
1 small red onion, finely chopped
Small pinch of five spice
Small pinch of cumin
2 tbsp chopped parsley
1 red chilli, finely chopped
1 egg, beaten

For the mixed salad
1 Romaine lettuce, washed and chopped coarsely
4 spring onions, chopped
6 cherry vine tomatoes, halved
6 sun dried tomatoes, roughly chopped
6 Borette or sweet pickled onions, sliced into quarters
12 anchovies in olive oil
6 slices of marinated peppers
4 sliced and marinated artichokes

Serves: 2 (one burger each is plenty)
Prep time: 30 minutes (lamb burgers should be made in advance and refrigerated to help maintain their shape whilst cooking)
Cooking time: 20 minutes

1 Place the lamb mince, breadcrumbs, red onion, five spice and cumin into a bowl and stir together mixing all through. Divide the mix in half and either place into cutter shapes or shape with your hands into a triangle, approximately 2cm thick.

2 Mix the chopped parsley and chopped red chilli together on a plate. Brush the sides of the burgers with the beaten egg and roll the sides of the lamb burgers in the parsley and chilli mix, covering generously. Refrigerate until ready to use.

3 Prepare the salad by simply mixing together all the salad ingredients in a large bowl.

4 About 15 minutes before you want to eat, preheat the oven to 180°C/350°F/GM4. (If you are making chunky chips it will already be on and the chips should be starting to crisp up.)

5 Using a non-stick pan, gently fry the lamb burgers on each side until nicely browned. I do not use any olive oil or butter as lamb has so much fat in already. I usually finish them off in the oven for approximately 10 minutes as I find they cook more evenly and stay moist in the middle. When ready, place them onto kitchen roll to blot off excess oil.

6 Serve and enjoy!

puddings

Parents often use the 'no pudding' threat to encourage their children to finish up their main course. But children don't always manage to eat the entire pudding either and lose interest, which is why I think puddings work best if they are fairly light and stodge free.

The puddings I have included here are a selection of recipes I have found most successful with my four. They are not massively into puddings and usually yoghurt and fresh fruit (a must!) does the trick, but at weekends I make a more extravagant pudding and we will all indulge.

raspberry meringue bomb

This is the easiest pudding recipe I know, and yet everybody assumes it must be very complicated and time consuming!

250g/8oz frozen raspberries
2 tbsp Crème de Cassis
280ml/10fl oz double cream
125g/4oz ready-made meringues

1 Start by defrosting the raspberries. Then push them through the mouli with a medium disk (or use a sieve and the back of a wooden spoon), squeezing out all the juice that you can. Stir in the Crème de Cassis.

2 In another bowl, whisk the cream until it just starts to thicken. I use a balloon whisk to do this – although it's tempting to use an electric whisk, you don't have the same control and can easily end up over-whipping the cream.

3 In a third bowl, crumble the meringues into quite chunky pieces. It is easy to be too thorough here – you want to achieve a rubble effect with lots of texture not dust!

4 Pour the cream over the meringues and mix up gently until the meringues are evenly coated.

5 Gently pour about half the raspberry couli over the meringue-and-cream mixture and stir in – but not too much. Ideally you want to achieve an almost marbled effect. Save the rest of the raspberry couli until later.

6 Pour the finished mixture into a 1 pudding basin, carefully cover with tin foil and put in the freezer for at least 3 hours.

7 When you are ready to serve, place the pudding basin in a bowl of hot water for about 30 seconds. Tip out onto a serving plate and cut into slices. Serve with the remaining raspberry sauce drizzled across each slice.

Serves: 6 children
Prep time: 15 minutes
Cooking time: 3 hours+

For the best results, this pudding has to be made in a very haphazard way!

mint ice cream with chocolate sauce

I always used to love mint-choc-chip ice cream, so I was determined to come up with my own version without the rather frightening luminous green mine used to be!

For the mint ice cream
300ml/½ pint milk
3 egg yolks
125g/4oz caster sugar
300ml/½ pint double cream
handful fresh mint, finely
    chopped

For the chocolate 'magic' icing
50g/2oz dark chocolate

Serves: 6 children, generously
Prep time: 30 minutes
Freezing time: overnight

1 Put the milk in a pan and heat until just boiling. Beat the egg yolks and sugar together and pour on the hot milk, whisking all the time.

2 Return the mixture to the pan and stir over a gentle heat until the mixture has thickened slightly and coats the back of the spoon. Remove from the heat and transfer to a bowl. Leave to cool completely.

3 Softly whip the double cream and fold into the custard mixture. Add all of the chopped fresh mint, stirring in gently. Place inside a Tupperware tub and put into the freezer.

4 After approximately 3 hours, take out of the freezer and softly stir the edges into the middle, as they will freeze first and doing this will ensure it freezes evenly.

5 Place back in the freezer and freeze overnight.

6 For the magic icing topping, break the dark chocolate into chunks and melt in a small glass bowl over a small saucepan of simmering water. Do not let the chocolate over-heat. Gently stir until it is all liquid.

7 Leave to cool and then drizzle over the ice cream when ready to serve. This will harden on contact with the ice cream — pop into the freezer if not quite ready to serve.

hot chocolate puddings

The great thing about these is that they need to be prepared in advance. Make the mixture at least 2 hours before you need the puddings and leave them on the side until it's time to pop them in the oven.

250g/8oz plain chocolate
125g/4oz unsalted butter
3 eggs
2 heaped tbsp caster sugar
1 tbsp plain flour
1 tsp vanilla extract

Serves: 6 children
Prep time: 15 minutes
Cooking time: 10 minutes

1 Preheat oven to 200°C/400°F/GM6.

2 Start by greasing 6 200ml overproof pots. Then put the chocolate and butter in a heatproof bowl above a saucepan of simmering water.

3 In the bowl of the electric mixer, whisk together the eggs, sugar and vanilla extract until frothy. Alternatively, use a large bowl and hand-whisk. Sprinkle over the flour and fold in.

4 When the butter and chocolate have melted, gradually add to the egg mixture, folding in with a large metal spoon.

5 Pour the mixture into the pots and leave to rest for a couple of hours.

6 Cook for no more than 10 minutes until cooked at the sides but soft inside. Serve with plenty of double cream.

frozen yoghurt

This is hardly a recipe, but it makes a healthy alternative to ice cream and, if you always keep a bag of frozen berries in the freezer, is a very good emergency pudding.

500g/1lb wholemilk bio yoghurt
400g/13oz frozen summer fruits
Maple syrup

Serves: 4–6 children
Prep time: 2 minutes

1 It couldn't be easier! Just put the yoghurt into the liquidizer jug with the frozen fruit (straight out of the freezer) on top.

2 Pulse for a few seconds until just puréed. Any longer and it all starts to melt.

3 Serve immediately with maple syrup drizzled on top.

crème brulée

600ml/1 pint double cream
2 tbsp dried lavender flowers
8 egg yolks
2 tbsp caster sugar + 3 tbsp for
   the top

1 Put a 1 litre Pyrex dish in the freezer before you start cooking.

2 Heat the cream and the lavender in a medium-sized saucepan but don't allow to boil. Take the saucepan off the heat, put the lid on and allow to infuse for about 20 minutes.

3 In another bowl, mix together the egg yolks and 2 tablespoons of the caster sugar.

4 Strain the cream and lavender through the muslin into the egg/sugar mixture and stir well.

5 Rinse the saucepan before pouring the custard into it. On a low heat, gently heat the custard, stirring all the time with a wooden spoon.

6 Do not take your eyes off the saucepan and never stop stirring. It will take at least 10 minutes for the custard to thicken to the desired consistency – you want it to be able to coat the back of the wooden spoon thickly.

7 When it is ready, take off the heat immediately and pour into the freezing cold dish as quickly as you can. This is usually quite a comical exercise as I try to get the dish out of the freezer with one hand while continuing to stir the custard with the other. It would be too upsetting to curdle it at the very last moment!

8 Leave to set in the fridge for at least 5 hours.

9 Remove from the fridge and sprinkle the remaining caster sugar evenly over the custard. It is possible to melt and burn the sugar using a very hot grill, but it is much easier and more successful (not to mention much more fun!) if you use a blowtorch.

10 Return to the fridge for 30 minutes before serving.

Serves: 6–8
Prep time: 25 minutes
Cooking time: 30 minutes
Setting time: 5 hours 30 minutes

trifle with real custard and mandarins

I think it is best to make this a day in advance. It gives the flavours time to develop and the Madeira time to infuse the dish rather than overpower it.

**1 packet trifle sponges
    (usually about 8 in total)**
raspberry jam
**390ml/13fl oz tin mandarins
    (drained weight 240g/8fl oz)**
**75g/3oz walnuts
    (optional – you could
    use almonds instead)**
4 tbsp Madeira wine
570ml/1 pint whipping cream
**6 egg yolks (saving the whites for
    meringues of course!)**
1 tbsp caster sugar
1 tsp cornflour
275ml/10fl oz double cream
**glacé cherries to decorate
    (if you must!)**

1 Slice the sponges in half horizontally and spread with jam. Sandwich together and cut in half vertically into fingers.

2 Drain the mandarins but reserve the juice.

3 Place the sponges in a large glass bowl and sprinkle with the mandarin segments and walnuts. Give it all a good mix.

4 Push the sponge mixture flat and pour over the Madeira. Then pour over a couple of tablespoons of the reserved mandarin juice. Clean the inside of the bowl with some kitchen paper and put to one side while you make the custard.

5 There is a great deal of mystery that surrounds making custard. Homemade custard is always spoken of in a whisper for fear that talking any louder will automatically curdle the whole thing and result in throwing a great deal of expensive ingredients down the drain. I shared this dread until somebody told me that by adding a teaspoon of cornflour to the eggs and cream, the mixture became considerably more stable and consequently the process was less likely to end in disaster. You still need to be careful, but as long as you concentrate and take things slowly, your sense of satisfaction will be huge!

6 So, to make the custard, heat the cream in a medium-sized saucepan. In a separate bowl, beat the yolks with the sugar and cornflour.

7 Don't let the cream boil, but when it is very hot, pour it over the egg mixture, stirring all the time.

8 Wash out the saucepan and return the custard to it.

9 Put the saucepan back on a low heat and don't stop stirring until it thickens. You will feel it start to thicken before you actually see it happening, but don't take your eyes off it or get distracted! It will probably take about 10 minutes.

10 Once it has thickened to a consistency that thickly coats the back of a wooden spoon, remove from the heat, but keep stirring – if you don't, the residual heat of the saucepan will overcook the custard.

11 When it has cooled slightly, pour it over the trifle base. Leave to cool for an hour before putting in the fridge.

12 Whip the double cream and, if you feel like some fun, pipe all over the top. Decorate with glacé cherries.

13 Take out of the fridge at least half an hour before serving.

Serves: 6–8 children
Prep time: 35 minutes

lemon and lime pots

This is a really light and refreshing dessert. Serve chilled as a lovely after-supper treat - it's great in the summer!

3 leaves of gelatine
25ml/1fl oz water with 1 tbsp
   caster sugar
500g/1lb crème fraîche
zest of 1 lemon
zest of 1 lime
150ml/5fl oz lemon and lime
   juice

Makes: 6 little pots
Prep time: 30 minutes
Chilling time: 2 hours+

1 Soak the gelatine in cold water.

2 Meanwhile, bring the water-and-sugar mixture to the boil in a small saucepan.

3 When the gelatine has gone soft, squeeze the leaves and dissolve in the water-and-sugar mixture.

4 Whisk the crème fraîche in a large bowl and add the zests and juices.

5 Sieve the gelatine mixture into the crème fraîche mix and stir through. Pour equally into small pots and put into the fridge.

6 Leave to set for at least 2 hours – or overnight. A great dessert to prepare in advance!

Tip

• Gelatine leaves are best, but if you can't find them, ordinary sachets of gelatine will work fine. Simply follow pack instructions against the amount of liquid the recipe uses – 175ml/6fl oz.

lemon and cranberry baked cheesecake

I find this is a much lighter cheesecake than the traditional one which my children find too heavy and rich. The dried cranberries add a lovely colour, although you can use any dried fruit.

For the base
50g/2oz softened unsalted butter
150g/5oz digestive biscuits,
    crushed into crumbs

For the filling
350g/11oz full-fat cream cheese
    (Philadelphia)
150g/5oz golden caster sugar
4 medium eggs
1 lemon, zest and juice
2 tsp vanilla essence
1 handful dried cranberries
300ml/11fl oz soured cream

1 Preheat oven to 180°C/350°F/GM4.

2 Melt the butter in a small saucepan.

3 Break the digestive biscuits into chunks and place into a food processor. Whizz until you've got smooth crumbs. Place into the mixing bowl and add the melted butter, stirring until all the crumbs are evenly coated.

4 Press the base mix into the bottom of a lightly greased 20-cm cake tin — this must be a tin with a removable collar. Press the mix firmly into the edges.

5 Place all the topping ingredients EXCEPT the cranberries and soured cream into a mixing bowl. Mix together until smooth and stir in the cranberries. Pour this mix on top of the biscuit base, bake for approximately 30 minutes until just set and remove from the oven. It continues to set while cooling.

6 After approximately 10 minutes, smooth the soured cream over the top. Replace in the oven and cook for a further 10 minutes.

7 Remove and allow to cool and set.

8 Remove the collar and slide off the base onto a serving plate. Place in the fridge.

9 Refrigerate until serving.

Makes: 12 slices
Prep time: 15 minutes
Cooking time: 40 minutes

meringues and chocolate

For the meringues
2 egg whites
100g/4oz caster sugar

For the chocolate
75g/3oz plain chocolate
100ml/3fl oz crème fraîche
100ml/3fl oz double cream

1 Preheat oven to 140°C/275°F/GM1.

2 Start by making the meringues. Whisk the egg whites in a large bowl until they make peaks that don't bend over when you remove the whisk from the mixture.

3 At this point, sprinkle one third of the sugar over the egg whites and very gently whisk in. Repeat this process with another couple of tablespoons of sugar. Sprinkle the remaining sugar over the egg whites and, trying not to knock out any of the air in the mixture, fold in with a metal spoon.

4 Using a dessert spoon, spoon the meringue mixture onto the baking sheet into individual mounds. Cook for 40 minutes.

5 While the meringues are cooking, melt the chocolate in a glass bowl above a saucepan of simmering water. When it has melted, stir in the crème fraîche.

6 In a separate bowl, whisk the cream until it has thickened slightly. Carefully fold the chocolate and crème fraîche into the cream.

Serves: 4 children
Prep time: 30 minutes
Cooking time: 40 minutes

7 When the meringues have cooled, sandwich together with the chocolate mixture and serve.

vanilla custard

It may seem strange to serve this as a dessert on its own - but I find it so comforting and delicious! The fantastic infusion of vanilla makes it quite refreshing.

1 vanilla pod
570ml/1 pint whipping cream
6 egg yolks
1 tbsp caster sugar
1 tsp cornflour

1 Place a Pyrex bowl large enough to hold a pint into the fridge to chill. This will help avoid any curdling disasters!

2 Scrape out the seeds from the vanilla pod and place in a saucepan along with the cream. Heat this together to a high heat but do not let it boil!

3 Beat the egg yolks with the sugar and slowly add the cornflour – this helps to make the mixture stable and less likely to curdle.

4 When the cream and vanilla are really hot, pour into the egg mixture, stirring all the time.

5 With your supposed other pair of hands (this is the tricky bit!) wash out the saucepan then return it to the stove and pour the custard mix back in. Put this on a low heat and do not stop stirring until it thickens – you will feel it thicken before you see it. This takes about 10 minutes.

6 When it thickens enough to coat the back of a spoon, remove from the heat but keep stirring.

7 Pour the custard into the fridge-cold bowl – this will stop it from overcooking or curdling.

8 Cool or serve immediately.

Makes: 1 pint
Cooking/Prep time: 30 minutes+

baked apples with currants and brown sugar

I used to love the smell of these cooking when I came in from school - just the smell of apples cooking now reminds me of that lovely comfort of coming home after school! The children love this dessert as well, as puréed apple was one of the first solid foods they had.

4 cooking apples
2 tbsp Demerara sugar
handful of currants
1 lemon, juice
4 knobs of unsalted butter

Serves: 4 adults or 8 children
Prep time: 15 minutes
Cooking time: 25 minutes, approximately

1 Preheat oven to 160°C/310°F/GM2½.

2 Core the apples carefully.

3 Lightly grease a baking tray and place the apples on it.

4 In a small mixing bowl, mix together the sugar and currants and stuff them into the centre of each apple.

5 Drizzle over the lemon juice and place a knob of butter onto the top of each apple.

6 Score with a sharp knife around the centre of each apple – this stops them bursting as they heat up.

7 Place in the oven for approximately 25 minutes, until you can see the apple has softened and the juice is coming out.

8 Leave to cool slightly.

Tip

• Delicious served with double cream, crème fraîche or ice cream!

rhubarb and peach crumble

The children love this - delicious rhubarb and the comforting, lovely honey flavour of roasted peaches topped with a fantastic crunch of roasted hazelnuts ...

For the fruit
4 peaches, washed
100g/3½oz soft unsalted butter
250g/8oz Demerara sugar
6 sticks of rhubarb
   (cut into 2cm dice)
2 cinnamon sticks

For the crumble topping
150g/5oz plain flour
1tsp ground cinnamon
80g/3½oz butter
80g 3½oz Demerara sugar
4 tbsp roasted hazelnuts

Serves: 6 hungry children
Prep time: 15 minutes
Cooking time: 35–40 minutes

1 Preheat oven to 180°C/350°F/GM4.

2 Brush the peaches in some soft butter then roll them in the sugar. I find this easiest on a tray to contain the sugar.

3 Place the peaches in a snug oven-proof dish with the cinnamon sticks and put in the oven to roast for approximately 20–25 minutes, until they can be easily pierced with a knife. Discard the cinnamon.

4 Meanwhile, roll the diced rhubarb in butter and sugar in the same way and place onto a baking tray. These will take approximately 10–15 minutes.

5 Take out the peaches, peel off the skin and remove the stones. Cut the peaches into 2cm dice. Remove the rhubarb from the oven and place with the peaches in the bottom of another oven-proof dish. Add all the juices from the baking as well.

6 Rub together all of the crumble ingredients (apart from the nuts) for the topping. Rub until it looks like fine breadcrumbs.

7 Crush the nuts in a bowl with a rolling pin then fold this into the topping mix.

8 Sprinkle the topping over the fruit, then bake for 20 minutes, until you see the fruit beginning to bubble up at the sides.

really easy fruit tarts

This is the easiest (and some would say tastiest) dessert of all! The tarts take no time at all to make and are a great way to use up fruit that has gone a little soft. Also very good for encouraging children to try different berries.

175g/6oz dessert pastry (shop bought)
plain flour to sprinkle on the work surface
8 tbsp mixed fresh berries (any combination – a mix of blueberries, raspberries and blackberries always goes down well)

Serves: 4 children
Prep time: 15 minutes
Cooking time: 25–30 minutes

1 Preheat oven to 160°C/310°F/GM2½.

2 Divide the pastry into four equal balls. Sprinkle the flour onto the work surface. Roll out the pastry (each ball separately) until about 5mm thick and in a rough square shape. Place 2 tbsp of mixed berries onto the centre of the pastry and fold up the sides to cover. Push the pastry together at the top.

3 Using a spatula, place onto a lightly greased baking sheet and place in the oven for 25–30 minutes until the pastry is golden brown and the berries are bubbling.

4 Be careful, they are very hot in the middle!

5 Serve.

Tip

• Great with a spoonful of vanilla ice cream or cream.

party food

Although children's parties can be a nightmare to organize they can also be great fun. I think the secret is to keep them as simple as possible and to plan everything in advance – I swear by writing lists!

Party food is particularly fun to make as you can relax the rules and be a little over the top. Again, I think it is best to keep food simple. Inevitably, there will be children there with different likes and dislikes to your children's so make sure you produce a good spread with a little bit of everything. That way everybody will be fed and you are less likely to have any tantrums on your hands.

The recipes I've included here are the ones that have gone down the best at parties we've held. They are all easy to make and cut as many corners as possible!

party survival tips

- Keep parties simple and forward plan as much as possible.

- Make sure you have a list of games to play and music to dance to at the ready. I find that old-fashioned games like musical bumps and musical statues always go down the best.

- Make up and label party bags in advance. Rather than filling them with lots of tiny plastic games, just get one or two items, such as a skipping rope and notepad and pen for the girls, and a wind-up car and a bouncy ball for the boys. The bags will take less time to prepare and should also be less expensive.

- Make a list of all the children at your party and ask parents to sign them in and out. It is very nerve-wracking to be in charge of a large group of other people's children and you need to be sure of who is where and who is collecting who. If you have rented a hall make sure you know the points of entry so no child can go without you knowing.

- Use disposable plates and cups. It makes cleaning up afterwards so much easier!

- Try to make it a rule that the children have to stay sitting down when they are eating. Running around is too messy and can even be dangerous.

- Never let your child start opening presents during the party – things will get broken and lost. It also makes it much easier to make a list of who to thank for which present.

cheese straws

This is one of those really useful items to have at parties - keeps little ones amused for ages and gives the older children something to nibble on while waiting for tea. I include the mustard powder because, as with the sausage rolls made in Lunch Bites, it adds a delicate kick!

75g/3oz wholemeal flour
60g/2½oz plain flour
125g/4oz butter, cubed
1 egg (separated)
60g/2½oz cheddar/parmesan
   mixed and finely grated
½ tsp mustard powder
1 tsp poppy seeds
1 tsp sesame seeds

Makes: approximately 25 cheese straws
Prep time: 15 minutes
Cooking time: 10 minutes

1 Preheat the oven to 200°C/400°F/GM6.

2 Rub together the wholemeal and plain flour with the butter until you've got fine crumbs. Add the egg yolk, all the cheese and the mustard powder. Mix together and then knead into a ball.

3 Sprinkle flour onto your work surface and roll out the dough to approximately 5mm thick.

4 Cut the pastry into straw sizes, approximately 1½cm wide and 15cm long. Brush over the straws with the beaten egg white and sprinkle each straw with either sesame or poppy seeds. Very gently, push them a little into the pastry.

5 Using a fish slice, place each straw onto a lightly greased oven tray and bake for approximately 10 minutes, until lightly golden.

6 Once cooked, remove immediately to a wire rack to cool and avoid overcooking the bottoms.

Tips

● These are also delicious made with a spoonful of basil pesto or tiny chunks of sun-dried tomato in the dough mix, adding great colour and flavour.

● The cheese dough freezes very well. Always store in an air-tight container to maintain freshness.

● Great in a lunch box, too.

pitta pockets

Children love pitta bread pockets: they are easy to pick up, fun to eat and it is always a lovely surprise to see what they are stuffed with. The advantage of this is you can sneak in hidden goodies.

400g/14oz tin of chickpeas
½ tsp cumin powder
¼ salami, cubed (I prefer Napoli
    salami)
6 spring onions, finely chopped
1 red pepper, deseeded and finely
    chopped
6 sun-dried tomatoes, finely
    chopped
2 tbsp coriander, finely chopped
12 wholemeal mini pitta pockets

For the dressing
½ lemon, juice
2 tbsp olive oil
2 tsp crème fraîche

1 Drain the chickpeas and mash gently with the back of a fork. Tip over the dressing and sprinkle on the cumin, then allow to marinate for approximately 10 minutes.

2 Add the cubed salami, spring onions, red pepper and sun-dried tomatoes and gently mix together. Sprinkle in the chopped fresh coriander.

3 Lightly toast the pitta fingers until just slightly crispy (optional), and gently slice open the top to allow you to stuff the inside with the chickpea salad.

4 Fill and serve.

Serves: 12
Prep time: 20 minutes
Cooking time: 5 minutes if you choose to toast the pittas lightly (optional)

pasta twist salad

This salad went down particularly well at the last children's party I held. It was the last of four parties in a row and I was fed up with wasting sandwiches that no one ate. There was not a single pasta twist left!

500g/1lb fusilli pasta
2 x 185g/6oz tins tuna chunks
   in oil
340g tin sweetcorn
3 tbsp mayonnaise
½ cucumber, cubed

Serves: 15 children as part of a table of party food
Prep time: 10 minutes
Cooking time: 12 minutes

1 Cook the pasta as directed on the packet –
   I love using fusilli for this pasta dish as it is
   easy for children to eat with their fingers and
   manages to hold some tuna flakes onto itself.

2 Simply drain the tuna and flake it gently in a
   mixing bowl. Add the drained sweetcorn and
   spoon in the mayonnaise. Mix together gently,
   taking care not to mush it. Add the cucumber,
   stir through the drained pasta and serve.

Tip

● Wholewheat pasta makes this a healthier option.

potato skins

12 potatoes weighing
  approximately 100g/4oz each
5 tbsp olive oil
salt and pepper

1 Preheat oven to 200°C/400°F/GM6.

2 Carefully stab the potatoes all over with a knife before rubbing a little of the olive oil into their skins.

3 Place straight onto the oven shelf and bake for about 40–45 minutes, until they feel slightly soft when squeezed.

4 Remove from the oven and allow to cool until you are able to handle them. Cut into halves lengthways and then into quarters. Scoop out the potato flesh inside, leaving a layer of about 1cm.

5 Place the quarters on a wire rack above a roasting tin with the skin-side facing downwards. Brush the surface with the remaining olive oil and season with salt and pepper.

6 Return to the oven and set the timer for 15 minutes. Remove from the oven and turn the potato skins over before returning to the oven for a further 15 minutes.

7 Allow to cool a little before spooning in the various fillings.

Serves: enough for about 20 children
Prep time: 15 minutes
Cooking time: 1 hour 15 minutes

potato-skin fillings

When cooking for a children's party it is essential not to spend too much time cooking intricate dishes which nobody is really going to appreciate. My potato-skin fillings are therefore handy 'cheat' recipes!

The quantities are enough to fill all the skins, when made together.

mild chilli and cheese filling

1 tbsp olive oil
½ tsp chilli powder
200ml/7fl oz frozen bolognaise
   sauce, defrosted
½ tin kidney beans
100g/4oz grated cheddar cheese

Prep time: 5 minutes
Cooking time: 15 minutes

1 Preheat oven to 200°C/400°F/GM6.

2 On a medium heat, warm the olive oil in a medium saucepan and stir in the chilli powder. Stir for about 1 minute before adding the defrosted bolognaise sauce and kidney beans.

3 Bring to the boil and simmer for 10 minutes before spooning onto the potato skins. Sprinkle with grated cheddar and return to the oven for about 10 minutes, until the cheese has melted.

Tip

- When I freeze my bolognaise sauce (see recipe page 154), I usually use 200ml freezer pots, the reason being that this is an ideal amount for two children and it also defrosts in an afternoon.

spicy baked beans and cheese

In an ideal world, you would be reaching for your freezer and retrieving a lovingly made tub of homemade baked beans (see Breakfasts), but in the real world, just reach for a tin of Heinz in the cupboard instead!

400g/14oz baked beans
1 tbsp Worcestershire sauce
100g/4oz grated cheddar cheese

Prep time: 10 minutes
Cooking time: 5 minutes

1 This is hardly a recipe! Preheat the oven to 200°C/400°F/GM6. In a small saucepan warm the baked beans, adding the Worcestershire sauce at the end.

2 Spoon the baked beans onto the potato skins – but drain off a large amount of the juice if you are using the tinned kind, otherwise they will be too sloppy. Sprinkle with the cheddar and pop in the oven for 10 minutes.

crème fraîche and chives

I think this tastes much nicer if you remember to get the crème fraîche out of the fridge a couple of hours before you need it.

1 bunch chives, finely chopped
400ml/14fl oz tub half-fat crème fraîche
½ lemon, juice
salt and pepper

Prep time: 10 minutes

1 Mix all the ingredients together and spoon onto the warm potato skins. Serve immediately.

cocktail sausages with honey and mustard

4 tbsp clear, runny honey
1 tsp English mustard
40 cocktail sausages
3 tbsp sesame seeds

Serves: 20 children
Prep time: 10 minutes
Cooking time: 20–25 minutes

1 Preheat oven to 180°C/350°F/GM4.

2 In a small bowl, combine the honey and mustard.

3 Put all the sausages in another bowl and pour the mustard and honey mixture over them. Very gently stir the sausages around until they are evenly coated.

4 Put in the oven and set the timer for 15 minutes.

5 After 15 minutes, remove from the oven and sprinkle the sesame seeds over the sausages. Give the baking tray a good shake to make sure they are evenly coated.

6 Return to the oven for a further 5–10 minutes.

7 Allow to cool before serving, because the hot honey will make the sausages somewhat hazardous.

egg mayonnaise bruschetta

1 loaf ciabatta
3 tbsp olive oil
6 large eggs
150g/6oz pancetta, cubed, or
    bacon lardons
3 tbsp mayonnaise
pepper
small bunch chives, finely
    chopped

Serves: 4 children
Prep time: 15 minutes
Cooking time: 15 minutes

1 Preheat oven to 200°C/400°F/GM6.

2 Slice the ciabatta in half horizontally, then slice each half into 2cm fingers. Place on a baking tray and drizzle with olive oil. Put in the oven for about 7 minutes until the bread has started to crisp and lightly brown.

3 In the meantime place the eggs in a saucepan, cover with water and bring to the boil. Simmer for 6 minutes. As soon as the eggs are ready, tip out the boiling water and pour cold water over them. When you are able to handle the eggs, gently crack their shells and leave in the cold water until you are ready for them.

4 In a frying pan, fry the pancetta until it is just beginning to crisp.

5 Roughly chop the eggs and combine with the mayonnaise, pancetta and pepper.

6 Spoon onto the ciabatta fingers, sprinkle over the chives and serve.

peppermint creams

These always remind me of sweets my grandmother used to have in her cupboard. Not a healthy option, but fine for a treat from time to time. I sometimes wrap up one or two in tissue paper with a ribbon to go into a party bag.

1 egg white
340g/12oz icing sugar, sieved
3 drops peppermint essence

1 Place the egg white in a mixing bowl and whisk until frothy.

2 Beat in about two-thirds of the sieved icing sugar and add the peppermint essence to taste (I find 3 drops is plenty).

3 Place the mixture onto a clean work surface and knead in the remaining icing sugar. Check the flavour again, adding another drop of peppermint essence if desired.

4 Split the mixture in half and shape each half into a long sausage shape, approximately 2½cm thick.

Makes: 36
Prep time: 30 minutes
Setting time: Overnight if possible, at least 6 hours

5 Dust a chopping board with a little more icing sugar, place the icing sugar sausage onto the board and cut the peppermints into about ½inch slices. Mould into perfect round shapes and place onto parchment paper, well spaced. Leave to set, if possible overnight but at least for 6 hours, to harden on the outside.

Tip

- You can always add a drop of food colouring to these as well, to make them slightly more eye-catching.

fruit jellies

This is cheating, but it's a fun and relatively healthy party pudding.

300g/10–11oz frozen blueberries
135g/4½oz pack blackcurrant jelly

1 All you really have to do is follow the instructions on the packet of jelly, but with a few modifications!

2 I break the jelly into cubes into the bottom of a measuring jug. Add boiling water up to the half-pint (285ml) mark and stir until all the jelly cubes are completely dissolved.

3 Tip the frozen fruit into the jug, which will probably bring the level to the 1 pint (570ml) mark. If not, top up to that level with cold water.

Makes: 6 small pots
Prep time: 5 minutes
Setting time: 3–4 hours

4 Spoon the jelly mixture into the six small pots and place in the fridge to set.

Tip

- The advantage of using frozen fruit is not only that it is cheaper than using fresh fruit (and in this particular recipe, I don't think anyone will notice the difference) but also that the jelly will set very quickly, so you don't have to make them the night before if you don't want to – or if you forget!

gingerbread lollies

I love these lollies - they are a great alternative to hard-boiled lollies and a great deal tastier! I like using heart- and star-shaped cutters but choose any shape you like.

200g/8oz plain flour
1 level tsp baking powder
2 level tsp ground ginger
1 level tsp ground cinnamon
75g/3oz unsalted butter
75g/3oz soft brown sugar
3 heaped tbsp golden syrup

Additional equipment
Lolly sticks
Shaped cutters

Makes: 20
Prep time: 25 minutes
Cooking time: 10–12 minutes

1 Sieve together the flour, baking powder, ginger and cinnamon into a large mixing bowl.

2 Put the butter, brown sugar and golden syrup into a small saucepan and place over a low heat, stirring until all the ingredients have melted and the mixture is all runny – do not allow it to boil.

3 Pour the mixture into the flour and, using a wooden spoon, mix all together until it becomes like a dough and easy to work. It may look a little greasy but this will even out when rolled out with flour.

4 Flour a work surface and roll out to just over 1cm thick.

5 Using heart and star cutter shapes, about 5cm in diameter, cut out your shapes and, using a palette knife, place onto a baking sheet lined with parchment paper.

6 Place into the oven at 180°C/350°F/GM4 for 10–12 minutes, until lightly golden brown. Do not overcook – they do firm up as they cool.

7 As soon as they come out of the oven insert the lolly stick into the base, at least 2cm in to be able to hold the weight of the lolly

Tips

● For a healthy option, gently push raisins or dried cranberries into them when they come out of the oven, before they firm up. These are lovely iced as well.

milk jelly

This may sound very strange, but as small children we preferred this way of making jelly to the normal method. It was creamier and also had a fascinating cloudy effect.

135g/4½oz packet orange or
    tangerine jelly
170g/6oz tin evaporated milk

Makes: 6 small pots
Prep time: 5 minutes
Setting time: 3–4 hours

1 Following the usual instructions, break the jelly up into cubes in a measuring jug. Dissolve with a pint (568ml) boiling water, stirring until the cubes have completely dissolved. Let it cool, then add the evaporated milk.

2 Pour into a glass bowl and put in the fridge until set.

chocolate peanut butter squares

This recipe does not need quality ingredients. In fact, I think it tastes much better made with Bourneville chocolate rather than fancy 80% cocoa solids stuff! This recipe includes nuts, so make absolutely sure there are no children at your party with an allergy.

100g/4oz plain chocolate
2 rounded tbsp crunchy peanut
   butter
3 cups Rice Krispies

Makes: 14 squares
Prep time: 10 minutes
Setting time: 2 hours

1 Lightly grease a square 22cm non-stick tin and line the base with baking parchment.

2 Melt the chocolate and peanut butter together in a bowl above a saucepan of gently simmering water. Stir well to combine thoroughly.

3 Remove the basin from the heat and carefully add the Rice Krispies until they are completely coated with the chocolate-and-peanut-butter mixture.

4 Spoon the mixture into the tin and spread around, pushing down evenly.

5 Put in the fridge for about 2 hours until set.

6 Turn out of the tin and cut into squares.

cinnamon and apricot fairy cakes

125g/4½oz unsalted butter
  (softened) for the sponge
125g/4½oz caster sugar
2 large eggs (free range, organic)
125g/4½oz self-raising flour
100g/4oz unsalted butter
  (softened) for the butter icing
200g/8oz icing sugar
2 tbsp milk
1 cinnamon stick
6 dried apricots sliced lengthways
  in half – soak these in Earl
  Grey tea with a cinnamon stick
  for approximately 5 hours

Makes: 12 cakes
Prep time: 15 minutes
(+5 hours to soak the apricots)
Cooking time: 15–20 minutes

1 Soak the apricots in a small bowl with the cinnamon stick and Earl Grey tea for approximately 5 hours. Take out and drain on kitchen roll.

2 Preheat oven to 190°C/375°F/GM5.

3 Place the butter and caster sugar in a mixer or beat by hand until the colour has become almost white. Add the eggs one by one, beating well, then fold in the flour.

4 Divide the mixture between 12 cake cases and bake for approximately 20 minutes, until golden brown and springy to the touch. Place straight away onto a cooling rack.

5 Meanwhile, beat together the butter (for the icing) and icing sugar, adding the milk until the mix is fluffy and spreadable.

6 When the cakes are completely cool, cut into the tip a circle shape about 5mm away from the edge and about 3mm deep. Remove the cut-out and place carefully to one side.

7 Fill the hole with half a teaspoon of butter icing and half an apricot. Smooth another half teaspoon of icing over the top of the apricot.

8 Cut in half the section of cake you cut out and arrange on top of the apricot and butter icing as fairy wings. These will secure as the icing sets.

Tip

• You can use any dried fruit as the surprise inside these fairy cakes, and soaking them in fruit juice also adds a delicious taste.

mini pavlovas

This is a brilliant way of using up frozen egg whites.

8 large egg whites
500g/1lb caster sugar
2 tsp corn flour
750ml/1⅓ pint whipping cream, whipped
100g/4oz strawberries (hulled and quartered), raspberries, blueberries

1 Preheat oven to 180°C/350°F/GM4.

2 Whisk the egg whites until they make firm peaks when you remove the whisk from the bowl.

3 Sprinkle about one-third of the sugar over the egg whites and whisk in. Repeat with the second third. With a large metal spoon, gently fold in the last third of the sugar and, once it is well combined, gently add the corn flour, continuing to fold it in carefully.

4 Using two dessertspoons, spoon the mixture onto the baking parchment. Aim to make the Pavlovas approximately the same diameter as a jam jar, certainly no bigger or they become too cumbersome. Using a spoon, make a large dimple in the middle of the meringue mixture (this will later hold the cream and fruit).

5 Place in the oven and immediately reduce the temperature to 150°C/300°F/GM2. Set the timer for 25 minutes, and when it bleeps, turn off the oven without opening the door. Leave in the oven until cool (or for at least 30 minutes) before transferring to a wire rack.

Makes: 25
Prep time: 20 minutes
Cooking time: 30 minutes

6 When you are ready for them, simply spoon a blob of cream into the centre of each meringue and sprinkle with a few pieces of fruit.

Tip

- Meringues keep incredibly well. If you want to get really organized, make them several days in advance and keep in an air-tight container until you need them.

boy's birthday cake

It has to be chocolate - lots of gooey mess and crunchy Smarties or crumbling Flake ...

For the sponge
125g/4oz self-raising flour
25g/1oz cocoa powder
1 tsp baking powder
150g/5oz unsalted butter
150g/5oz Golden caster sugar
1 tsp vanilla essence
3 eggs
2 tbsp cold water

For the icing
150g/5oz plain milk cooking
   chocolate
145ml/5fl oz double cream

Serves: 12
Prep time: 20 minutes
Cooking time: 25–30 minutes

1   Preheat oven to 170°C/325°F/GM3.

2   Sieve together the flour, cocoa powder and baking powder into a large mixing bowl, then add the butter, sugar and vanilla essence, followed by the eggs. Add cold water and mix until you have a smooth dark brown mixture.

3   Divide this equally between two lightly greased and lined 18cm cake tins, knocking the tin on a hard surface to get a smooth top on each.

4   Bake for approximately 25–30 minutes, until you touch the centre and it springs back up – also you will see the sponge slightly shrinks from the sides of the tins.

5   Remove from the oven, take out of the tin and place on a wire cooling rack.

6   While it's cooling, make the icing. Break the chocolate into small pieces and melt in a small bowl with the cream over a saucepan of boiling water, until you can stir it into a thick, brown mixture.

7   Once the chocolate sponge is cool, place one half on a plate and spoon approximately half of the chocolate icing mix onto the top. Place the second sponge half on top of this and use the rest of the icing to smooth over the top – be generous! It doesn't matter if it runs down the sides – looks all the more indulgent!

girl's birthday cake

Very pink and pretty - you can never have too much pink!

For the decorations
1 red rose
1 white rose
2 egg whites
sprinkling of caster sugar

For the sponge
225g/9oz unsalted butter,
    softened and diced
225g/9oz golden caster sugar
225g/9oz self-raising flour
2 tsp baking powder
4 medium eggs
100ml/4fl oz milk

For the filling
150g/6oz raspberry jam
180ml/6fl oz mascarpone

For the topping
175g/7oz icing sugar
1 tbsp water
1 tbsp lemon juice
1 drop red food colouring
    (I find this pink deep enough,
    but adjust to your specific
    shade!)

Serves: 12
Prep time: 30 minutes
Cooking time: 45–50 minutes

1 The frosted petals are best done the day before. Gently break open the white and the red rose and remove the smaller and most perfectly shaped petals. I usually use about 6 petals of each.

2 Lay them onto a tray and, using a pastry brush, brush them with egg white on one side only. I do not do the other side of the petal as I find it makes them lose their shape and they look pretty enough like this! Lay them back onto the tray and simply sprinkle over the caster sugar until they have a lovely frosted look. Leave overnight in a warm place to dry.

3 Preheat the oven to 170°C/325°F/GM3.

4 Lightly grease two cake tins. They should be 20cm across and 9cm deep with a removable base.

5 Place all the sponge ingredients into a large mixing bowl and stir together until you have a nice smooth and creamy mix.

6 Tip this all into the cake tins, evenly divided between the two, and smooth over the top.

7 Place in the oven and bake for 25–30 minutes, until the centre of the sponge rises to the touch and the cake shrinks in a little around the edges.

8 Remove from the oven, run a knife around each tin edge and slip out. Slide the sponges off the bases. Leave on a wire rack to cool.

9 Spread the raspberry jam over the top of the bottom half. Be generous!

10   In order not to get into a huge mess, rather than topping the jam with mascarpone I tend to layer this onto the bottom of the top half, again generously, and then sandwich the two halves together.

11   Mix together the ingredients for the icing. The water and lemon juice give it a fresh taste and keep it from being too sickly sweet. You may add a little more water if it is too stiff. Add the food colouring for the desired shade.

12   Carefully smooth the icing over the top of the cake.

13   Arrange the rose petals on the top, carefully pushing them slightly into the icing so that they stay in place. Leave to set. A pink dream!

playdough

I know, this isn't edible - but I have learned from experience that being able to whip up a load of playdough on a rainy afternoon can be a real life-saver! Children seem to find it very relaxing and quickly become absorbed in their creations. It is fun watching their models become more and more sophisticated as they get older, and listening to them explain the parallel world of which they are Master.

These are approximate measurements and may need a little tweaking depending on the absorbency of the particular flour you are using.

2 cups plain flour
1 cup salt
1 cup water
food colouring
2 tbsp sunflower or grapeseed oil

1 Put all the dry ingredients in a large bowl. Make a well in the middle. Pour the water, food colouring and oil into the well and, using a metal spoon, gently start to stir the liquid around. The flour will start to collapse into the water and oil and become incorporated.

2 Once you have mixed it all together, adjust the quantities if necessary by adding a little more flour if it is too sticky, or more water if it's too dry.

3 Turn out onto a lightly floured surface and knead well until the food colouring is evenly distributed throughout the dough.

Tip

- It will keep for a couple of days in the fridge if you wrap it up very tightly in a sandwich bag or clingfilm.

a bit about vitamins and minerals

What	How	Where
Carbohydrate	Carbohydrates provide us with energy.	
	'Simple' carbohydrates should be kept to minimum, as they are a source of quick energy but have little other nutritional value. Don't forget tooth decay, too!	Sugar, honey, jam
	'Complex' carbohydrates are plant-derived, starchy foods that sustain us. These should form the major part of most meals.	Flour, bread, cereals, pasta, rice, potatoes, pulses, sweet potatoes
Fibre	Fibre is only found in food from plants.	
	'Soluble' fibre helps reduce cholesterol (a main cause of heart disease) and controls blood sugar levels (important to avoid and control diabetes).	Oats, beans, fruit, vegetables
	'Insoluble' fibre makes you feel full and prevents constipation.	Wholemeal bread, brown rice, wholegrain pasta
Fats	A small amount of fat is essential for energy and warmth. However, there are good fats (HDLs) which should be enjoyed, and bad fats (LDLs) which should be avoided. As a rule, 'saturated' fats are solid at room temperature and are consequently used to bulk up processed food. A diet high in saturated fats increases harmful cholesterol in the blood, causing damage to arteries and the heart.	Fatty meats, cheese, cream, butter, lard, cakes, biscuits, pastry
	Unsaturated fats (mono-unsaturated and poly-unsaturated) reduce levels of harmful cholesterol.	Olive oil, avocados, olives, seeds, nuts
Omega 3 & Omega 6	Omega 3 and Omega 6 are particular types of poly-unsaturated fats which the body is unable to make itself. The only way our bodies can get these essential fats is by eating them.	Vegetable oils, polyunsaturated margarine, mackerel, herring, salmon, trout, seafood, tuna, fish oil
Proteins	These are essential for growth and development, therefore children need diets higher in protein than adults. Protein is made up of amino acids, some of which cannot be made by the body and so have to be supplied by diet.	Milk, cheese, yoghurt, meat, poultry, fish, eggs, pulses, beans, nuts, bread, cereals, tofu
Calcium	Particularly important for growing bones and teeth	Milk, cheese, sardines
Iron	Essential for blood functioning and to avoid fatigue	Eggs, liver, beef, cocoa powder, dried fruit, green vegetables
Vitamin A	Needed for healthy hair, skin, nails and vision. It also keeps the immune system healthy. Too much, though, can be harmful.	Butter, margarine, cheese, eggs, herrings, sardines, almonds, peanuts

What	How	Where
Vitamin B group	Essential for a healthy metabolism, the process by which the body turns food into energy. Therefore, without the B vitamins children will not grow as well as they should. The body cannot store these vitamins, so it is important to eat these foods every day.	Wholewheat bread, marmite, beef, pork, bacon, cheese, fish, pulses
Vitamin C	The body needs vitamin C to repair tissues and resist infection. It increases your body's production of infection-fighting white blood cells and antibodies, and ups your levels of interferon, the antibody that coats the surfaces of cells, stopping viruses from getting in. Vitamin C cannot be stored by the body and can be lost by overcooking food. It is also an important antioxidant which may help prevent some cancers and heart disease. About 200mg of vitamin C a day will boost your immune system, so make sure you eat at least six portions of fruit and vegetables a day!	Fresh fruits and vegetables, especially blackcurrants, lemons, oranges, grapefruit, Brussels sprouts, cauliflower, cabbage, parsley, tomatoes, lettuce, strawberries, spinach and kiwi
Vitamin D	Without vitamin D the body cannot absorb calcium properly; it is also essential for healthy bones and teeth. Our bodies can make vitamin D when exposed to sunlight.	Oily fish, eggs, milk, butter, margarine
Vitamin E	Vitamin E is another antioxidant and can help protect the cell membranes and body from free radicals. A great immune-booster. It also enhances the production of B cells – lymphocytes that produce antibodies and help destroy harmful bacteria.	Vegetable oils, seeds, nuts, grains, cold-pressed oils
Folic acid (Folate)	We need folic acid to make red blood cells and maintain a healthy nervous system. It is essential in the early stages of pregnancy to prevent spinal defects in the embryo.	Green leafy vegetables, orange juice and marmite
Betacarotene	Betacarotene increases the number of infection-fighting cells, as well as being a powerful antioxidant.	Fruits, nuts, seeds, vegetables, particularly the orange ones – squash, orange peppers, sweet potato and pumpkin
Zinc	Zinc is a mineral which increases the production of infection-busting white blood cells. The body absorbs zinc more easily from animal sources than plant ones, so vegetarians should consider adding nuts and seeds to their diet.	Beans, wholegrain cereals and turkey
Selenium	Selenium boosts the immune system.	Cottage cheese, prawns, eggs, tuna, wholegrains, vegetables, brown rice, chicken, sunflower seeds, garlic, Brazil nuts, lamb

kitchen equipment

These days you can buy all sorts of weird and wonderful kitchen gadgets but whilst they might look nice they aren't always terribly useful. Here is the list of the equipment you will need to make all the recipes in this book. Don't worry if you don't have some of the equipment on the 'luxury' list, elbow grease will be just as good in most cases!

Essential equipment

Apple corer
Biscuit cutters (assorted shapes)
Casserole dish (assorted sizes)
Chopping board (ideally one for meat and one for non-meat)
Colander
Fish slice
Garlic press
Handheld blender
Handheld juicer
Handheld grater
Jars for storing pasta/rice/spices (assorted shapes and sizes)
Kitchen scales
Kitchen timer
Knives (assorted sizes and blades)
Little circular whisk
Loaf tins (assorted sizes)
Muffin tin
Non-stick frying pan (small/medium/large)
Ovenproof dishes (assorted sizes)
Palette knife
Saucepan with lid (small/medium/large)

Scissors (just for food)
Sieve (ideally small and large)
Slotted spoon
Spatula
Vegetable peeler
Vegetable steamer (in a stack over a bottom pan)
Whisk
Wire cooling rack
Wooden rolling pin
Wooden spoon
Zester

Luxury equipment

Bread machine
Deep fat fryer
Electric blender
Ice cream machine
Juicer
Kitchen aid
Mouli

acknowledgements

Biggest thanks go to Megan, Jack, Holly and Matilda for always eating so well and enabling me to try out different dishes on you all; Luke and Jessica often join in, Luke being particularly vocal when he doesn't agree with my ideas! Helen and Diane, you were also fantastic tasters and the best in-laws I could have asked for.

Thank you to my mum, you have always inspired me with your fantastically relaxed way with cooking, and I know you find it hard to write down recipes for me as they are all in your head and you instinctively know amounts without measuring! Olly, my sensible sister who is always rescuing me when I need someone to look after the children or indeed me!

Alex, your help with this book was amazing. You are my fellow mum of four who still bothered with me after my initial look of boredom when you asked the 'have you got twins?' question. Thank you – without your help I would have sunk.

Thank you to the dream team, Jenny, Wei and Deirdre – I think we have covered most topics of conversation during our shoots!

Susanna, thank you for pushing me, we got there in the end. Jacqui, you have done an amazing job, I love it all.

Finally, to Gordon – thank you, for always not interfering.

index